AFFIRMED:
Life Lessons In Racial Healing And Transformation

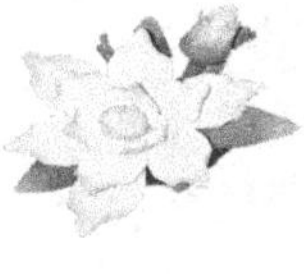

SHELI TURNER

ZEBERT PRESS

AFFIRMED:

Life Lessons
In
Racial Healing
And
Transformation

ZP
Zebert
Press

ZP Zebert Press

ZEBERT PRESS
5042 Wilshire Blvd., Suite 261
Los Angeles, CA 90036

For information regarding rights, bulk purchases or for bookings: info@sheliturner.com

Designed by MG Turner

Manufactured in the United States of America

Library of Congress Control Number: 2018908774

ISBN-13: 978-1-7325806-0-2 Paperback
ISBN-13: 978-1-7325806-1-9 Hardback
ISBN-13: 978-1-7325806-2-6 E-book

DEDICATION

To my mother and father, without whom
I would have no story.
To my husband and sons, without whom
I would have no one to tell it to.
To my stepmother and sister, without whom
I would have no witnesses.
To my brother, without who
I would have no adventure.
To each of you, with immeasurable love.

CONTENTS

CONTENTS (CON'T)

AFFIRMED:

Life Lessons
In
Racial Healing
And
Transformation

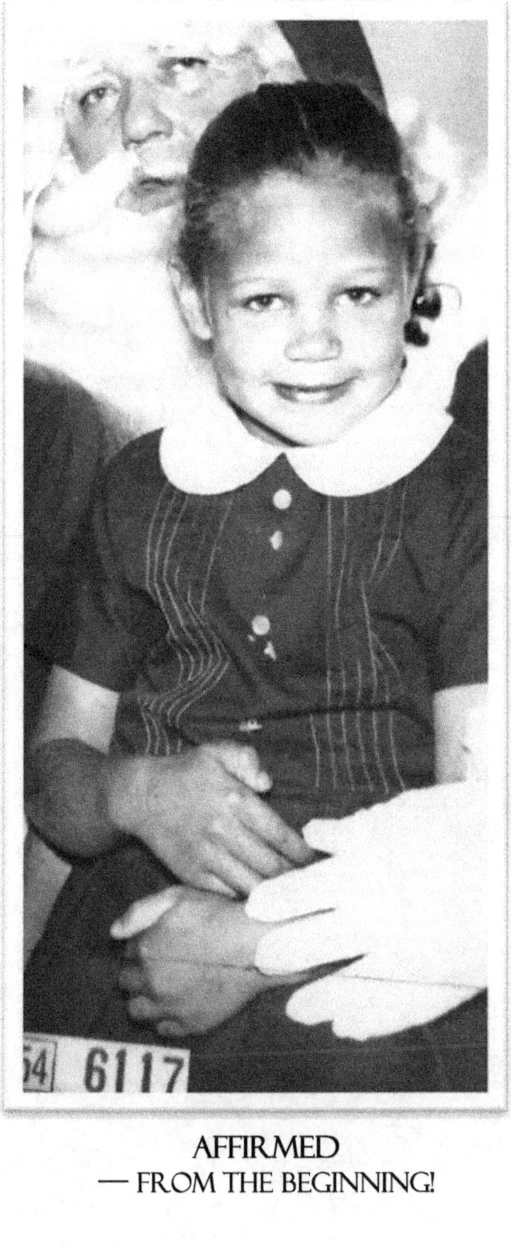

AFFIRMED
— FROM THE BEGINNING!

PRELUDE: APOCRYPHA

Don't look at me like I'm some saint.
I'll tell you what—
I ain't.
I've many untold stories.
I harbor confessions unheard.
Don't seek to hand to me your glories.
There are others who are better served.
My heart has stones I've cast and thrown.
Some at those I've loved and known.
Each end of day brings Grace to me
That I can forget the complexity
Of hurt I may have caused in my turn.
I yearn for peace of mind.
I burn.
The woman I am now has learned
There is no hurry in the moment.
Only truth.
I seek dearly to learn how
The salves of wisdom
Can anoint the wounds I've torn in my youth.
My hair isn't grey.
My soul, old, is.
Grey is not a saintly color.
Yet it is hallowed enough to patch
These ragged holes in my shoes.

BIRTHRIGHT
LESSON 1: INTENTION

My opportune birth was joyfully documented just minutes after Bastille Day, in a small general ward of the old historic French Hospital in San Francisco. In commemorative fashion after nine strenuous hours of induced labor, my mother named me Mary Michèle. My wild auburn hair and healthy lungs announced that I was not to be ignored, as if the resonances of liberation were to valiantly course through my veins, despite the fact of my actual delivery being a few minutes past the hour of a new dawn. Although I have never used my first name, Mary, was given to me both as the shortened version of her name, Rosemary, and as an acknowledgement of how my mother feared I would be tested. Mary means "rebellion." I was hers. Gravitas aside, I would be incessantly teased and mocked on the schoolyard playground with the saccharine lyrics of the popular 1967 Beatle's hit song, "Michelle." But righteously, I would be vindicated resoundingly each time the stirring echoes of Hendrix's "The Wind Cries Mary," was played at home on high volume. Like its clarion call of a premonition, the yearning, invincible energy of those soul filled words painted me perfectly.

My twenty-two-year-old mother's intrepid fall from grace was complete not only because she eagerly married my father, but because I was so proudly allowed to burst into the world. I was born prior to the 1967 Supreme Court ruling based upon the Loving vs. Virginia case, which legalized White and Black interracial marriage. Implicitly, the 19th amendment also legitimized their children, therefore my context for existence was for some time shamed without law. On both my father's and mother's sides however, I was technically not the first mixed-race child. As was common for the territory, my father's mother's parents and grandparents were typical local Appalachian mixtures of Cherokee Indian and White, and were never slaves. When her mother married a mixed Cherokee and Black man, my grandmother was legally registered as Black. Like many indigenous people of Virginia in the 1920's, the Racial Integrity Act forced families like hers to forsake their tribal affiliations and identification, especially when they intermarried or were mixed with Black, to remain in Virginia. My paternal grandfather had a differing palette for Black however, as he was connected directly as a descendant of slaves from an old Virginia family. My grandfather's mother was a tall, dignified West African woman, but we have no record of her native origin. Her "husband" was rumored to be the son of the slave owner, with distinctive blue eyes, a family trait still found today. My grandfather, along with his eight brothers and sisters, sharecropped the land they lived on, but it was my grandfather who would be known as the family workhorse. He would only be allowed to complete the sixth grade, having to forsake his opportunity to go on to study at Tuskegee Institute when offered a full scholarship, because his father strictly demanded he remain on the farm. With great diligence and vigorous grit, my grandfather would later send a younger brother to attend seminary school at Yale. Indeed, although he remained in the area, he became celebrated as the most able and pleasant businessman throughout Kings Mountain. He owned several houses that he solidly refurbished and rented to Black families, owned the juke joint and the Black cemetery—but also had to deal with the collection of Black money, or rather the non-collection of it, receiving only what people could pay him. My grandfather was no loan shark, and his kindness and benevolent understanding were long revered and remembered.

My mother's families endeavored to guard their sanctity of bloodline more vigilantly. On my grandmother's side, delineated ancestry, and strongly held anecdotes, clearly allege that I am descended from Virginia and North Carolina's oldest, and most notorious first families. One of my supposed ancestors held the governorship of North Carolina, twice, and was brazenly known as the Confederate Governor. My grandmother's cousin was also the second wife of Woodrow Wilson, who some say was the "first woman" President. Yet pertinent and circular to my history, is that her husband, a pious Virginia Democrat, ushered in Jim Crow in the North, and among other things, encouraged the introduction and passage of discriminatory legislation, such as a bill passed by the House that made interracial marriage in the District of Columbia a felony. He was a staunch believer and supporter of eugenics sciences, which were incubated at his alma mater, the University of Virginia, and also later used as the foundation for Nazi Nuremberg Laws. These adopted theories and beliefs eventually would become operationalized at the Virginia state level--most auspiciously as the 1924 Racial Integrity Act which was enacted to prevent racial mixing. This hushed, buried, rarely discussed law definitively protected and insulated Whiteness in Virginia--where the little known "Pocahontas" clause allowed proof of less than one sixteenth Indian blood to grant an exception for Edith

Wilson herself, protecting her racial purity, since she claimed kinship with Pocahontas or did little to dispute it. Despite grandstanding, hints that my grandmother's family branch was actually clandestinely Melungeon or regionally related were annoyingly whispered. It is true that the family name showed up on the census dockets of Melungeon family names identified in the early 20s to "out" families who were passing as White, when actually they were not racially pure. The family name also showed up on Indian survey rolls of those wishing to register for recognition in the Cherokee nations. It was my grandfather who, in a flippant jest that lingered throughout their forever married life, bestowed upon my grandmother the name "Helen Highwater." He said he did this to honor her beguiling high-cheek-boned beauty. He also had her personal stationary emblazoned with her Indian name, upon which I would dearly receive many a cherished, assuring, loving, correspondence.

My grandfather's family, on the other hand, were strident Welsh immigrants. His parents, aunts, uncles and cousins were haphazardly gathered together alongside my grandfather's brother and sisters to endure harsh travel over and through the Blue Ridge mountains in horse drawn covered wagons. They were in search of coal mining work and better lives, and easily settled with affinity in the valleys of Virginia and West Virginia.

Discounting calamities of race, my impetuous parents fled from Greensboro, North Carolina in the late March winter of 1958, (where my father was attending college in his sophomore year at North Carolina A & T, and my mother was working as a nurse), to be married in Brooklyn, New York. With money wired from my Yale uncle, now a minister who also arranged for them to be married secretly in the apartment of a friend, the two caught a train immediately after being forewarned at campus that they had been discovered. Their brave and cautious journey was circumscribed by travel in separate cabins to San Francisco. Once there, they looked forward to living protected by an unobtrusive and respectful governmental recognition of their authorized marriage, without prosecution or the threat of lynching. As my father would plainly elucidate to us however, the Loving Law was never equitably applied when it was ratified, and he never trusted it. "Understand that the case reached the Supreme Court because Loving was a White man," he would say. "A Black man would be foolish to think he was ever out of harm's way."

My parents were the ultimate young idealists, whom naively believed they would see racial reconciliation established as the outcome of the Civil Rights movement they strongly identified with. My younger brother and I were not their experimental examples, but their evidence to the world that peace could be so. They socialized with many friends in San Francisco whom were also interracially married and like-minded. In fact, I grew up in such a cocoon that I believed for years this "normal" was normal. But I was to learn ruthless lessons before I reached the age of thirteen that our normal was horribly offensive to the outside world, and that collateral damage could be seriously inflicted as a result. Of my parents' vibrant circle of interracial couples that constituted our comfort zone of dearest friends: one committed suicide, one was murdered with his throat slashed, one died of an accidental overdose, and adding to these insults, the weaknesses of my parents were not spared. I still remember each of these anguishing heartbreaks, and now have the hindsight to place them all within the contexts of a hypocritical, unforgiving society, disapproving of their struggles to maintain dignity and civility while living on this fringe.

Whatever could be salvaged as residuals of their ideals carried my parents through to their second marriages and "do over" friendships. My stepparents were both godsends to my mother and father, and each provided them healing and love. My stepmother brought her wonderfully confident Nubian goddess vibe to the household, channeling a "Black is Beautiful" connection that uplifted and fortified our family, especially with the marvelous present of a new baby sister. My stepfather was a firm no-nonsense, self-made guy, whose demanding work ethic mirrored my father's, and who enjoyed and embraced the happiness of two additional children along with his own daughter. The second time around, my parents were not in mixed-race marriages. These extended relationships heralded years of novel experiences for my brother and me to examine the safeguards of accepted social constructs, to curiously, fearlessly, dive deeper into cultural understanding on both sides, and to realize that while racialized sensibilities may have mattered to others, those same perceptions still mattered nothing to us and never changed our world view about the delicate shell of humanity.

Throughout their lives, my parents remained true to a strict admonishment of other people's prejudices, despite the side-effects of emotional scarring and onerous taxations personally. My father was not necessarily an easy person for others to know immediately, but when he did let his guard down, he became the most humorous, witty, droll and brilliant conversationalist. My mother's personality was one of the sweetest imagined, however she was surprisingly a bold and direct woman. She would sometimes share a story about how she would have to be introduced twice to someone new before she engaged a friendship. The first time, where predictably the other person perceived her as being a beautiful, accomplished and privileged White woman, and the second with their dawning realization that she was happily also the wife of a Black man, and loving mother of his children. Before they retired, my mother was a regional hospital management administrator and my father had a well-travelled career as an international nuclear design engineer. Retired, they both settled back into the impressive homes they inherited from their parents, and sought to regain lost connections with the slower and gracious paces of life they fled from in their youth. Sadly though, on several latest visits, my parents took pains to make it clear to me they knew they would die without their prized dream attained. With impending old age and oncoming elderly sensibilities, each had come to reluctantly accept this inevitable fate, nearly breaking my spirit. W.E.B. DuBois wisely and aptly surmised, "...The problem of the twentieth century is the problem of the color line." Surely, he could not have known how remarkably his prophecy would be twisted, evolving into something more fiercely nuanced. Painfully in this early twenty-first century, the unexpected but highly complementary paradoxes of multiracial and multicultural alignment with that color line are just as difficult calls to action.

On the other hand, I know who I am, and what my claim by birthright is. I am aware of the expectation I have been charged with by my sedulous parents. In an age where open and unadulterated conversations about racism and cultural expression could be therapeutic, narrow thinking remains the more common opiate for the masses, but not for me. My indisputably lived proof of concept instead is that "Affirmation" is the most forceful weapon to disrupt and destroy the monstrosity of racism. I am a woman that has exemplified a life with an unapologetic freedom of mind and soul--due to being powerfully Affirmed. When faced with racist gaps of moral will at the hands of others, I know with great conviction that only "Affirmation" is what unflinchingly allows an individual to prevail while waiting upon justice.

My mother passed away last Christmas, and I am slowly coming to terms with profuse silences, reminiscently in contrast to our conversations multiple times a day. Ironically, she portended her greatest legacy would be the stable survival of my brother and I in this same world that ravaged her life so greedily with unchecked imprudences of racism. To honor her, I am driven to share lessons gained in self-discovery: as a young girl, student, corporate professional, entrepreneur, academic administrator, daughter, wife and mother. It is my hope to empower others to willingly anticipate crucial idiosyncrasies of a fast rising multiracial and multicultural world. Secondarily, I wish to create an appropriate awareness, veneration, and empathy concerning the realities of those trendy portrayals of multiracial couples and their families colliding throughout media today. These images exist only due to dear human costs, and history should not be rewritten to romanticize this fact.

Unlike my parents, I will not be enshrouded by a calloused acceptance of a life in vain. In fact, it pleases me often to think of those ancestors whom would be rolling in their graves if blessed with the knowledge that their worst nightmare was personified by me, an arrogant cousin. It will be a magnificent, rowdy gathering of all of us when the Rapture comes, when we shall meet each other eye-to-eye, toe-to-toe. Thus, in order to prepare for a last stand against the price paid for history, it is with great intention that I cautiously place the lessons of honest memories, sentiments and encounters, as sacred burnt offerings upon the crossroads of crisis and sabotage that my family has never been able to run from.

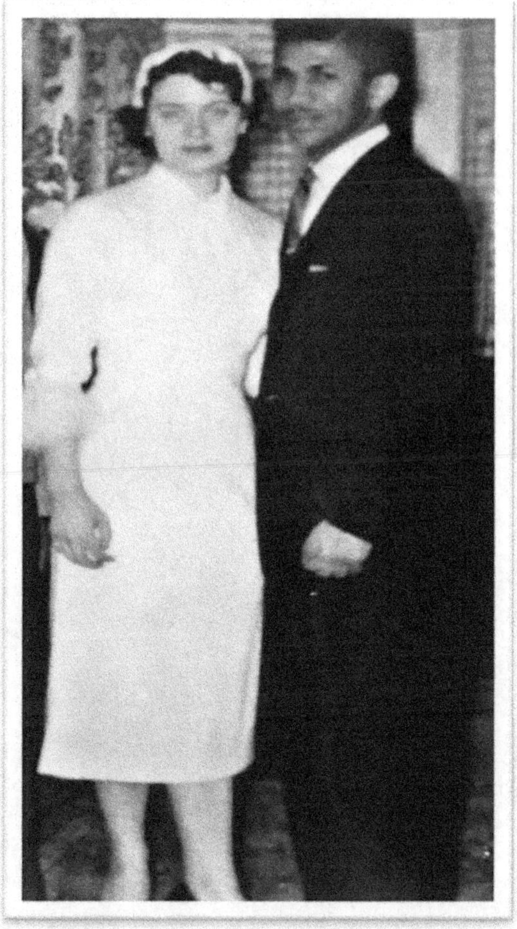

MOM AND DAD ON THEIR
WEDDING DAY: MARCH 22, 1958,
BROOKLYN, NY

MOUNTAIN SPEAK
LESSON 2: DECISION

I was ultimately brought to meet my mother's parents for the first time when I was a year old. My infuriated grandparents would not come to Mohammed, so my father decided after two years he would confront them on their own turf. Frankly, I believe they would have wished instead to come to San Francisco had they foreseen his viewpoint. At the time, Piedmont Airlines was the only air transport in the region, so we three tolerated the prop plane journey, albeit separately. My mother held me in her arms sitting several rows in front of my father. They had auspiciously determined that this was the safest and wisest way to travel. When we landed, her former roommate from nursing school picked us up in a white Oldsmobile station wagon. She of course knew the way to my grandparents' house from visits there often. With my mother and me in the front seat, and my father and luggage in the back seat, she carefully drove the single lane mountain highway with a watchful eye.

It was a beautiful three-story brick home in the middle of the block, on a quiet country street. My grandfather built his craftsman inspired house in 1927 with his own money, after also building the more traditional colonial home next door where my great-grandparents lived. My Aunt Mary also lived next door on the other side, and my Uncle Carl next to her. I would meet all of them on this visit.

Once parked curbside, it might have seemed most plausible to believe that it was my mother who got out of the car first and knocked on the door of the house she grew up in, but instead it was my father, who at the age of 23, long and lean, knocked on the door of his in-laws' house. And it was my grandfather who answered the door, instead of my grandmother. My mother, her friend, and I were still in the car. I was getting chilly in a little yellow bunny snowsuit, with the afternoon growing late and the sun falling behind the mountain peaks, but my mother would not yet move.

However, as soon as the heavy oak door opened, my grandmother was right behind my grandfather, peering over his shoulder. My grandfather was a heavy-set, big-boned, six-foot-four White southern Republican, salt-of-the-earth upstanding citizen. He had twinkling green eyes, but they did not twinkle at that first sight of my father. My father was just a bit shorter at six-foot-two, but dared to look him evenly in the eye, held out his hand and said with great measure, “Hello, Sir. I’m Louis. Rosemary is in the car with your granddaughter.”

At this, my grandmother deliberately shoved my grandfather out of her way, and keenly rushed to the car. She was crying, my mother was crying, and she reached in for me. In the next instant, my grandmother swept me into the house, leaving my mother in the car still, and my father still at the door. My grandfather would not be moved. He looked grimly at my father and being a man of few words, said simply, coldly, "Son, you and I are going to take a ride." Uttering nothing else, he strode briskly past my father down the front porch steps to his car parked in the driveway. It was a pale-yellow Lincoln, with a white steering wheel and matching interior leather. Gruffly and still silent, he slowly reversed out of the driveway to the middle of the street and grunted to my father to open the door and get in. As they drove off, my mother meekly stepped out of her seat finally, kissed her friend good-bye, and walked quickly into the house. My grandmother was sitting on the living room davenport waiting. From the window, my grandfather and father were becoming a distant picture in slow motion, already having turned the corner heading north toward the avenue. My father would know later to say that the top of East River Mountain was their destination.

As it has been told to me, the drive was heavy with a hostile lingering silence, bruisingly laden with unsaid epithets and my grandfather's pungent cigar smoke. Frustrated and incensed, my grandfather perilously challenged the curves of the mountain roads because of his familiarity with them, but also certainly with an intention to alarm my father. It worked. My father believed there was an inevitability that he was to be strung up in the mountain woods somewhere and left for the crows. When my grandfather was sure that he had reached his destination, he jerked the car to a skid and stop. At the top of East River Mountain, you can see the world. Nothing but treetops from West Virginia to Tennessee it seems, where the sky is jagged with green. Back then, there was no paved parking, just dirt clearing. My grandfather turned off the ignition at the ridge of the overlook. At the sound of that clank into stillness, my father reached for the door handle, ready to run because at the same time my grandfather was swiftly reaching under the front seat, and my father heard the rattle of a paper bag. He saw a glimmer of something that my grandfather deliberately pulled out of the bag, which in seconds was a pint bottle of whiskey, or, rather two. One he grabbed for himself, and the other he tossed at my father. Still without words, and not looking at my father next to him, my grandfather looked over his steering wheel at the waning horizon, turned the screw top loose and started swigging several gulps of Jim Beam bourbon, which in fact was his drink of choice until he died. In between each gulp were garbled words flying at my father, inflamed with entitled racist disgust, self-righteousness and fatherly indignation: "You Black son-of-a-bitch!" "Goddamn you Boy, I could choke you with my bare hands!" "Get your Nigger Ass out of my sight and out of this town, and leave my daughter alone!" ...were some of the remembered phrases. My father froze in his seat, in fact he removed his hand from the door handle and willed himself to calmly contain the fury that had begun to rage within him too. He looked at the bottle in his lap and noted the coming of dusk over the mountains. He too twisted off his cap, and also swigged several gulps although bourbon was not his brand, but he could hold his own. And he fired back: "You White cracker bastard!" "You don't even know me!" "I don't need a motherfucking thing from you or your kind!" "You lay a hand on me, and I promise you they will have to find us both cold and dead in the morning!"...My father exhausted himself with anger, but he was alert for the fight. Surprised, my grandfather sat up straighter, wiped his brow with his pocket handkerchief and took a quick stock of this young Black man in his car shouting at him, something he had never encountered before in his life. At my father's pause, he said quietly, "We should be going." My father wound down but did not reply. It was dark now. They had been on that mountain for nearly two hours drinking and cursing. My grandfather turned the key in the ignition, and instinctively started the car down the road in pitch darkness.

These hillbilly woods were the same that my grandfather's family had come across in a covered wagon at the turn of the century, so he knew them well. But he passed the turnoff to his house, and instead kept going until he reached the town center, stopping in front of a men's retail shop.

"Louis, you come on, now," he said with short order. My father was bewildered. "What the Hell?" Cautiously, he bit the filter off the broken cigarette he found in his pocket, lit it because he was nervous and followed. Inside, as the shop owner deferentially approached, my grandfather nonchalantly lit up a new cigar. "Mr. Burton, so wonderful to see you this evening!" the owner said welcomingly. "What can I do for you?" He had friendly eyes for my grandfather, totally missing that my father was standing there too, in fact, totally dismissing him. "Well now Earl," my grandfather puffed unhurriedly. "I need to buy three new suits and have them fitted so that I can get them picked up by tomorrow." "Certainly sir, of course!" "Well…" my grandfather continued, "that will be right fine. Now listen, I know that it might be short notice, and that it's almost time for closing, but you're sure that won't be a problem?" "Oh, no Mr. Burton! I can have them ready. I have your measurements on file, but I just need to take a minute to confirm your waistline— "

"No, Earl not for me," my grandfather loftily gestured with the cigar. "For him. For my son-in-law."

Needless to say, Time stopped. The eager shop owner had never waited on a Negro, but in that next instant he did so, because he had to. My grandfather was the head of just about every civic lodge in that town: Masons, Shiners, and Elks. He was someone not to be doubted or fooled with. "Earl," my grandfather said, this time with command as he sat down to wait for my father to be taken care of, "I want those suits delivered tomorrow, you hear? Oh, and make the bill to the house." So, my father had his measurements taken, which for him was just as much a surreal experience as for the man who had to do it. A White man had never waited on my father, and although it felt foreign, my father determined then it would not be the last time.

My grandmother once again gingerly rushed onto the front porch when she saw the car approaching. "Merciful Heavens, Charles!" she exclaimed, "I was worried sick!" "Now Mother," was the patient conciliating reply, "you needn't have worried."

My father did not go into the imposing house immediately. He sat on the porch swing until my grandmother shooed him inside. "Don't catch your death now son, come inside. I have supper waiting." "No, Mrs. Burton, I will be on my way. I was going to drive to my parents' home tonight and not stay here. I'm not trying to put anyone out, and honestly I would be more comfortable if I didn't stay." My mother was in the kitchen, but she came out when she heard this. "Okay then, I am going with you."

"Nonsense, you will both eat supper, and you both will stay here!" This time, it was my grandfather bellowing. He had come upstairs from the basement garage, huffing a bit from having hurried. "What's all this! No one is going anywhere anymore, damn it all!" In the same flurry, he surly demanded, "Where is my grandchild? Bring her to me!"

My grandfather had a favorite chair in the sitting room. It was a big mahogany piece of furniture that I used to love to crawl into because it smelled of his cigars and spicy cologne. In this chair, he tenderly cradled me for the very first time. I don't know what he said to me, or what he thought about me in those first moments, but I do know that I never wanted for anything after that. He loved my brother and me dearly, and we became his greatest joy. Whatever my father and grandfather, two proud men, had to put aside, we were the benefactors. They grew to have a respectful relationship that lasted even after my parents divorced. My grandfather conceded that my father was to be accepted as the head of his family. And being one head of family now mutually dependent upon the grace of the other, the contested privilege of color or race dissolved in importance.

For his part, my grandfather took care to teach me one of the most significant lessons that has sustained me still: "You are supposed to be in the room." As I grew up shadowing him, I had various random but important assignments. I was his money counter on poker nights. I put the offering in the plate at church on Sundays. I was his junior chef during visits in the Fall, and chief elf during many Christmastimes when we would personally deliver his homemade fruitcakes to the shut-in families. He never made excuses to his friends about his grandchildren, and never failed to include us everywhere in his circle. He loved to take us to his office and show us off to his employees every time we came to town. He spoiled us rotten from the youngest ages. When we were in elementary school, we had a candy account established at the market that we could charge whatever we and our friends wanted. When I was in high school and college, I shopped in the best of stores, and had my things delivered with receipts only to him. As I got older, he would cannily ask my opinion on stocks, news and his favorite race, the Kentucky Derby. With such an unchallenged upbringing, I believed surely that I was absolutely supposed to be in the room because there was no good reason why I should not be. Not one that mattered, and not one that would cause me defeat.

Consequently, effortlessly I observed, learned and understand the unspoken language of White people, which, was precisely my sly grandfather's objective. I am instinctively familiar with their thinking, coupled with an immediate sensitivity to their habits of entitlement and privilege. Thus, I can most easily discern their nuanced and rapid degradations of comfort levels when having to engage with individuals from groups they feel do not deserve their indulgence or equity, especially Black. My grandfather prepared me well, and he was always proud of me. He felt strongly it would never be the case that I would ever encounter my better, and he made sure I knew it also. We were a dynamic duo.

When my grandfather became ill with cancer, he had one simple request of me when I came back home his last summer. I packed our lunch and we drove up to the top of the East River Mountain, a favorite place. He told me the story again of how he and my great aunts rode in a wooden covered wagon for three days to cross the mountain into Bluefield. He said that the hills were covered in blue flowers, which is how the small town got its name. I had heard the stories numerous times. "You know little gal, your father and I came up here a long time ago. I am sure he has told you the story." "Yes, he did, Grandpa. When he tells it, he says you hated him, and I can never believe that part of it."

"Believe it…believe it. Back then, I had such a revulsion in my heart because that was just the way I had been brought up. And that night I realized your father detested me too. I could see it steaming out of him, and I heard it in his voice when he cursed me." I said nothing, letting him continue. "And then I realized even with all that rage, your father refused to fear me. It made me look at him differently. It made me look at myself differently as well, and I didn't know what to do with how I felt. So, before we came home, the best I could do was to take him downtown and I bought him three new suits to show him that I was not his enemy. I didn't quite know what I was going to be, but harboring hate for him wasn't going to change anything. Somehow, I became convinced he loved your mother, enough to defy me no matter the cost. And on top of all that, there you were! Your grandmother let me hold you, and I felt like God was talking to me! You were that magic key! I hope you have always known that I could never imagine the goodness of my life without you or your brother in it."

We sat there for a long while, because we both loved the beauty of the vista. The rustle of the wind in the trees, and the soft meandering sounds of the river far below were familiar, casting a wondrous reverence upon my grandfather's life journey. Indeed, he had seen everything from horse drawn wagons, to men walking on the moon, yet was somehow one to unfold the many progressions of his experiences, to include that perhaps he did not need to hear the words to Sly Stone's latest album deafeningly if he just closed the basement door! My brother and I ruled the playroom downstairs each summer because his aim was that we felt secure and happy in his/our home. Grandpa had seen civil rights and social justice pursuits so unusually personally, that he fiercely grappled with having to let go of his indoctrinated beliefs time and again. But he clearly understood his risk was one of a future with loss, most notably after those first two years estranged from my mother. Successively, my grandfather opened his heart, mind and spirit to unforeseen and profound enjoyment, immensely provided because of his grandchildren. My grandfather decisively contributed tremendously in shaping the manner in which we engaged the world. His was not a natural social evolving, but a determination absolute, which sincerely defined the wisdom he imparted to us.

I recall delicious times when we would drive up the mountain roads to search for cat-tails from around the boggy freshwater streams for my grandmother's floral arrangements, or simply come up for a ride on the train at the top of the ridge because it was too hot in the valley below. But this afternoon we were glad to take our time to eat grilled cheese sandwiches and drink root beer, beholding an astounding view through the mountain haze. No words could describe the splendor of what we had negotiated and shared together as a family. I could not have had a more magnificent relationship with my grandfather, because his life by unambiguous intention and example prioritized those he loved.

In deference to the chastening revelation that changed him forever, my grandfather often drove alone to this place. Here he could listen pensively to the speak of the mountains around him, and humbly acknowledge the omnipotent presence of a God greater than any fleeting courage found at the bottom of a bottle of bourbon.

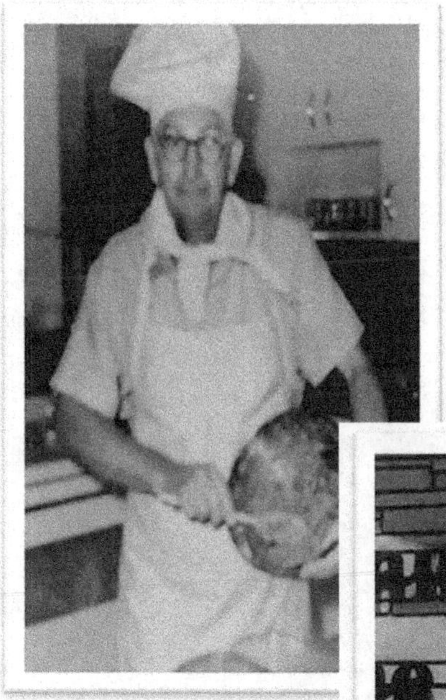

GRANDPA CHARLIE
MAKING HIS
ANNUAL XMAS
FRUITCAKES.

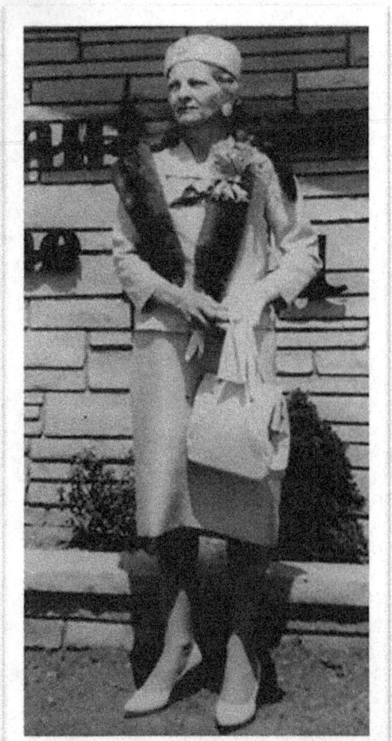

GRANDMA HELEN
DRESSED FOR TEA.

FLIGHT
LESSON 3: LOVE

I clearly remember that bracing, expansive feeling of flight. I was soaring, legs kicking and whipping on the wind as I glided and plunged on my swing. Hair captured as rope braids thumped and stung the back of my neck when I swooped mightily over the other crying runny-nosed toddlers. My days and evenings at nursery school were proscribed dutifully from swing to swing. Not knowing the difference between birds and myself, kinship with the shrieking seagulls was carefree and rambunctious. I could smell the ocean from the playground. I loved breathing the crisp tangy air in between swishes up and down. As the swing lifted me up and over, toes pointed skyward in flight, I could see the white crests of the ocean waves on the horizon.

"Daddy pushed me so I could fly!" I shouted, jumped up and down, and stamped my patent leather Mary Janes. "Daddy pushed me so I could fly!" In quick, short breaths, my discovery and telling was urgent.

"What in the world are you talking about, you silly thing?" My mother had come to pick me up after working her night shift at the downtown hospital, and being somewhat tired she could not easily interpret my state of condition. In response, I was puzzled. She of all people knew I was certainly no idiot child. As she proceeded to explain to me that my father had been at work all day, I was insistent and nearing exasperation. I threatened a tantrum because I wanted my mother to believe me and indulge my truth.

My beautiful mother, logical but now curious, explored a remote possibility that someone had conceivably pushed her daughter on the swing earlier. She quickly flushed, becoming worried however, because there was no other adult man authorized to be on the nursery school grounds. Troubled, she marched with small, concerned, mincing steps to the administrator's office. Every teacher's aide was called in to mollify her. One by one, each extolled how cute, how smart, how precocious her baby was, but each of those women absolved that she had not been near the swing-set that afternoon. Miss Mary was the last to come in. When I saw her, I went electric. "Daddy pushed me! See!" Happy, hot tears streamed on my cheeks. I waited for the agitated look on my mother's face to change.

And it did, although slowly, to a knowing, familiar look. My mother and Miss Mary hugged. "Thank you," my mother quietly said, her voice warm and calm. "There, Mommy do you see?" "I told you Daddy pushed me! And I like her very much, don't you?" "Princess," my mother muffled into my hair, carrying me out of the office to our fabulous white Ford Falcon, "you cannot call her Daddy anymore. You have to call her Miss Mary from now on, okay?"

I was truly perplexed by now, but I said, "Okay." But then I added, "Why?"

"Because only your Daddy is Daddy." Every person has their own distinct name," my mother explained to me reassuringly and buckled my seatbelt. "You must be sure to use the right names from now on."

I knew I had not gained satisfaction. I sighed an, "Okay" again heavily, and curved myself piteously around my favorite pillow left earlier from the morning's drop off. We were now going to pick up my father from work. I watched the foggy San Francisco streets roll by, thinking that I could not wait to see him. As soon as I spotted him standing on the corner of his office building, I could not get out of the car fast enough. I was charging his knees, shouting "Daddy!" With a small, almost defiant turn of my head, I could spy my mother standing beside the open car door watching and smiling.

Later at home, dinner plates floated on the wafting smells of our Chinese takeout meal, our regular during the work week. "Louis," my mother's voice interrupted the melody of chiming forks and chopsticks. "We had an incident today at nursery school. The baby said that her Daddy pushed her on the swing today, yet I knew you were at work. I was worried to death, but you know what? The mystery has been solved!" "Miss Mary pushed her!" My mother and father then began laughing uncontrollably, dropping their chopsticks, not able to swallow their food. I blinked at them both incredulously. What just happened?

In my beginning, I reasoned that the entire world was made up of "Daddys" and "Mommys" just like mine. I was proud that I could now easily classify individuals by common things, just like I thought I saw everyone else doing. I did not yet understand the necessity to additionally include characteristics pointlessly attributed to cause further distinction, like everyone else actually did. I had innocently relished time spent with a lady that was kind and loving to me just like my father was, so I believed the labeling was appropriate. I was naming love, not merely color. Still, by the time dessert was served, I began to sense the simple imperfection of my logic. I swallowed my chocolate pudding and the idea that Miss Mary should never be called "Daddy" again, although her soft skin was the same comforting red velvet brown. Growing older, minutes and years from that moment, I reasoned astutely that dazzling new flights above the world could become more byzantine. As fate would have it without question, these adventures would swoop me higher and plunge me deeper than those caring hands which pushed me, far and away beyond the unassuming distant ocean landscapes I once connected with, birdlike, from my nursery school swing.

A DANCE WITH WHO BROUGHT ME

LESSON 4: IDENTITY

I was born and raised in San Francisco not because of any coincidence, but intentionally, as a matter of my life or death. Other than survival, it is hard for me to imagine that my parents had a sane plan when they got married and fled from their childhood Virginia homes to San Francisco. But they thought they could safely escape. In March 1958, they eloped to Coney Island. After a non-stop treacherous drive in the middle of the night from Greensboro, North Carolina, they were married in the living room of a friend of my uncle's in Brooklyn. Like most romantic children, they stole off into the night. But like most lynching candidates, my father navigated nervously with the shadow of the South behind him. The Brownie snapshot taken on their wedding day depicts my mother standing with my father in front of a nondescript brick fireplace, with a pillbox hat neatly on her hair, which incidentally in this picture is dyed jet black. My mother is looking directly at the camera, a defiant Mona Lisa smile upon her face. My father looks courageous and determined. Other pictures of that day show my father standing in a distance on the boardwalk at Coney Island, the snow falling softly upon his long tweed coat, flakes dusting his hair stylishly parted on the side. I know my mother took that picture because my father is posing, trying to look dashing and impressive.

My mother is the first fragmented piece of my childhood. I see bits of her that shine and glimmer in my memory, but they are small with sharp edges. I remember little of my mother and father married. But this is because of memories that shout at me when I crack open that closed door in my brain, like the one of me struggling to pull a kitchen chair over to the counter so that I could reach the stovetop to make my brother and myself breakfast when I was eight years old. My mother was passed out upstairs in her bed, and he was hungry. I took a box of oatmeal and poured it all into a large pot, filled it with water, and turned on the burner. I found the wooden spoon and stirred the oatmeal until it bubbled. I went back into the pantry and found the sugar and put it on the table. I set two bowls out and found the butter and milk in the refrigerator, and then mixed them into the oatmeal the best I could. Finding a TV tray on the bottom kitchen shelf, I arranged a bowl for my mother, and uneasily stepped a cautious climb up the stairs. I woke my mother up to eat, shaking her mercilessly. I do not remember the mess I probably made on the kitchen counters, the stove, the floor, nor do I know who ever cleaned it.

One Christmastime, there was a party up the street at my mother's best friend's home, so we all walked instead of taking the car. Everyone could hear the music blaring out into the street, with the voices of the neighborhood overflowing out of open balcony windows into the holiday of the evening. It grew late, but I was not ready to go home just yet, and I ran into the kitchen to plead with my mother to let me stay and play longer.

When I reached the kitchen doorway, I saw that my mother must have just fallen backwards in her chair, already drunk, and so I watched quietly and unobtrusively as those standing around tried to help both my mother and the chair back up. I knew from the look on my father's face that it was time to go, and that come hell or high water, he would get my mother to walk that sidewalk back down the street. I can't quite remember when I got into my bed that night, but I do remember that the hot flush of anger and embarrassment followed me into dreams for many nights after.

There was also the time when one bright afternoon, my mother came to pick my little brother and me up from school. She must not have been quite stable enough to make it home, proving it by driving our red Volkswagen in a manner that challenged death. We sometimes were on the wrong side of the street, or on the sidewalk curbs, or the streetlights turned red and we went right through. My mother must have also driven over something on this wild ride to cause a tire to blow out. The car veered and dangerously swerved, and horns were loud blasts around us. I tried to take the wheel from her to steer, but I was only nine. I could not fathom the mechanics of driving, so I just closed my eyes. I opened them to flashing red lights and police sirens.

One of my last memories of my mother and father together is when I got out of the car in the parking lot of an old pink building, squeezing my father's hand. Once we were inside, I followed him down the hall past rooms that were filled with people I did not recognize, with sounds of people I did not know. I was led into what seemed to be a large hospital room with my godfather standing sadly in it. Becoming instantly alarmed, I ran to wrap myself into the shelter of my godmother's Chanel No. 5 hug. I gazed over at my mother who was sleeping in a bed near a window, and then tiptoed to wake her. She dreamily opened her eyes, but she did not know me. It was the medicine my mother was being given, I was told. It must have been a most high degree of chemical combination to take my name from my mother's lips.

Soon thereafter, my Grandmother Helen came to visit. My mother's mother was an elegant, delicate, fiery southern woman whom few could order around. She was a formidable contender, able to withstand word sparring with my father. Indeed, they were nearly evenly matched. Each had a command of presence, and a definite look in their eyes that set jaws tightly when control of tempers or situations was needed. They were also both smokers then, and often during this time, intense discussions would be swept up into a rhythm of decisive shoes pacing floors, with waves and rings of smoke clouding and hanging as right hands would signify conversations with growling voices.

Imagine then my surprise when my serious-minded grandmother cheerily offered the idea of a trip for all of us to Disneyland! All of us together! We would pack up the car and drive from San Francisco to Anaheim, making several visiting stops along the way. My brother and I had been bought and sold with the idea. We were delirious when our car finally rumbled down the steep hill of our driveway, pointed south. Driving leisurely from San Francisco, we first stopped in Carmel and toured the mission. I saw seals in the bays below the cliffs all along the coastal highway. Redwood and cypress trees were tall, splintered dark green, and bent into the misty winds, yet when south enough the trees morphed into palm fronds and orange groves unimpressively. After a difficult night of excited sleeping and waking, and sleeping but waking again, we embarked upon the glorious gates of Disneyland, grandmother in tow. The skies were so clear that the Matterhorn Mountain was magnificently glistening. The day was luxuriously steeped in masses of Pirates of the Caribbean jewels, and to add to the wonderfulness of it all, my grandmother bought us everything we saw. By the end of the day, I had as much treasure as any pirate! Grandma loved the day as much as we did. She sang, "It's a Small World" with a southern lilting twang enthusiastically the entire afternoon, and much of the ride back. When we got home, my brother and I quickly dumped our treasure, and ran outside to tell the neighborhood bunch about our great adventure. But later that night, I learned that only my brother, my father and I had unpacked. My grandmother and my mother were taking a train back to Virginia in the morning. I simply do not remember how I could finish dinner after eating this news, go to sleep, wake up, go to school, stop crying.

After several years, my father recounted that I said I hated him that night. I agreed that it was highly probable that I did say that, since being a very blunt child, I wasted few words on fewer people. When the lock of my arms was broken from around my mother's neck, and then a runway and then a sky separated me, there was little left to be said. The words of childhood choked in my throat, and I doggedly refused to count the years that I said goodnight to my mother dressed in a wooden picture frame. I stonily never saved her letters or remembered the weekly telephone conversations, because I wanted no reminders of the distance that carried them. Yet, I learned to keep loving and believing in something I could not see or touch. And I waited three long amorphous years for her heal, and to remember that her decision to love us against all odds was worth the cost of her frayed and desperate soul. When she returned to us, she told me that even the best trapeze artists needed to have a strong safety net underneath. She had free fallen without one and had endured the best way she could. To her guileless credit, my mother valiantly had commandeered our little household for several years working double nursing shifts, day and night, before my father would be professionally hired as a design engineer, finally, in 1966. Due to the new Civil Rights legislation, he was able to quit his job as a waiter, although he held an engineering degree. Simultaneously, Mom was responsible for answering to the needs of two small children and keeping a functioning home. Unspoken too, was the weight she carried because of her commitment to my father and to their efforts to normalize their lifestyle choice. With all of this, my mother had little resistance to the highs and lows from the pills she was given by her physician colleagues to keep her up so that she could work, or to the alcohol to bring her down which was dispensed with good intentions at first from her friends and then with bad advice. Of course, I was too young and could not rationalize the folly of my mother's oncoming addictions. Regardless, in these rough and toxic waters of my childhood unsettled by exhausted motherhood, I tried to look for a steady and safe harbor. To little avail, I lost hope my family could be rescued because we were on our own, going under, with no support system nearby to offer or share a lifeboat.

As devastating as our storm was with the wrenching of my mother from our home, my father would often break catastrophic solemnness with explosions of laughter. He had now assumed the role of family cheerleader. "I love ME! Yes, I do!" he would confidently declare to an audience of two standing in the mirror, awaiting final morning inspections. "I love ME!" A grin, a gleam, a sparkle in his eye set the tone for our day. "We love you too!" we would shout right back. "You see, you really have to love YOURSELF," he would continue. "You just have to LOVE yourself because I promise you, one day you'll wake up to find out that someone's trying to knock you on your ASS!" My father swore like a sailor, but that was ordinary to us. We were never given the privilege however.

"Do YOU love YOU?" he would challenge, taunting us. "Yes, I love ME!" I would loudly reply and giggle at the thought of it. At some usual point in his inspection, my father would spit into his hands and rub them firmly down the combed part in my head. This was to smooth out the flyaway hairs sprouting from my pigtails that he had brushed each morning. Next, he would turn to my brother and spit and smooth out the part in his hair also. "You know, I am PRETTY too!" he would add. To be sure, my father was handsome. Every morning without fail we would find him dressed in a suit and tie, with a white shirt that he had pressed the night before. He ironed our clothes also each night as part of our evening routine. My brother's pants had the kind of crease down the middle such that they could standalone by themselves, and my dresses were always store rack perfection. "You two monsters are pretty too because you are my 'Chilluns'—but I don't know if you'll ever be as pretty as ME!" Honestly, he blessed us this way every morning.

It seemed a wonder to all who observed that our father "raised us up." At the ages of nine and seven, our mother was gone, and my brother and I did not know if we would ever get her back. But our father was there in full force. He washed our clothes, took the two of us to Sunday school and church, shined our shoes, cleaned our house, grocery shopped, cooked our food, had two jobs, and never complained. On Saturday mornings, he would fix and flip pancakes and watch cartoons with us. On Sundays, it was maple French toast. He was there somewhere in the front row for school assemblies or choirs or plays, swimming in a sea of mothers. He would wash our hair, and every day got up early enough to comb and braid mine before breakfast. With timed precision, our breakfast done, he would hurriedly swallow his coffee and head on out the door, with a jaunt in his step to catch the cable car. My brother and I would watch him until he faded into the distance, turning the corner. He was on a furious mission.

Most summers during school break, my brother and I would go back to Virginia and daydream and play for two months. In the house that my father grew up in, I could lie on his childhood bed and faintly see through the large paned windows the outline of an old building under the trees at the top of the hill. When my interest got the best of me, I would easily cross the fields into the high grasses and wander over to the burned ruins that had once been a brick schoolhouse. In the evening, it became a large, looming evening shadow, seeping and staining the bedroom walls. In his past, my father, small and six, would brace himself for the bite and chill of the mornings, and walk in a direction with that same schoolhouse against his back to catch an old diesel bus that would take him forty miles, passing and stopping in several towns during the first lights of sun break. No matter how sleepy or aggravated with the cold he would be, he would step off that bus and through the only ramshackle doorways that were designated to tolerate and teach the county's Colored children. My father and his cousins all went to the same school together, their pathway to education simplistic, coded, generational. Those school bus rides marked the passing of their lives into adulthood, with drivers never sympathetic to their fledgling aspirations or yearnings. At a young age, I was informed about why they traveled so far, and I exactly understood also that the burned school building, which was merely a short walk away at the top of the hill, represented my family's sufferings from the loss of justice. It was for the town's White children only.

My father did not speak much about the tribulations of being Black in small town Virginia, but it was communed in the air we breathed in synch together, whether we were in Virginia or San Francisco. Accordingly, my father did in fact meet each day as a personal battle. In the mornings when we three stood in front of the mirror, my assurance was his image that met us from the other side. It would look back with a loving smile of confidence, a gleam of retaliation, a hint of divine mischief. To be sure, my father and his alter ego in the mirror were conscientious agitators, and once he was ready to go in the morning, he loved nothing more than to challenge himself brain to brain with the White man. My father was an engineer who designed nuclear power plants. Despite his Virginian segregated elementary and secondary school education within the county line, and a racially limiting college education that originally dissuaded him from his dreams, he escaped. Despite being told that his course credits from the Black college would not be accepted for transfer, he started over and graduated from the University of California at Berkeley. Each and every day, he readied himself as a more than able man. With a perfunctory revenge, my brother and I became his chess pieces. As we grew up, given every prized achievement, he would move us strategically on the path he envisioned to checkmate, enabling our success, therefore his success.

For decades now, I have stood on my own in front of my own mirror, with my memory sharply reminiscent of how he would leave us each early morning with his "Goodbye, be good!" kiss still wet on our cheeks as he hurried down the street. My brother and I would watch him from our front door until he became small in the distance, yet, this man was the biggest man our hearts could ever imagine.

My parents were probably too young for marriage, and it is only remotely possible they may have been wrong for each other. Left to a life isolated from their families, they could not offer each other needed stability in times of danger or trouble, largely because they both had the kind of personalities that strained and stressed the edges of conventional social boundaries. They both had genius IQs, and both were self-centered enough to believe they could outsmart the times they lived in. In those days, everyone relaxed with a scotch or bourbon glass in one hand and a cigarette in the other, and unmistakably the generation itself was experimenting with cross purposes.

My parents were beautiful, exceptional people, but found most of life surrounding them to be unconquerably insincere and frigid. Truthfully, they were living ahead of their time, out of their time. My truth, ascending from my parent's example, is that time and love are colorless. However, I have nowhere to reconcile the senselessness of how this same wonderful veracity caused our household to come undone, and I honestly do not know what could have prevented chaotic spirals throughout their lives or mine. I hold faith that at the end of Time, I shall be able to look back at it all, and be done with wondering or blame.

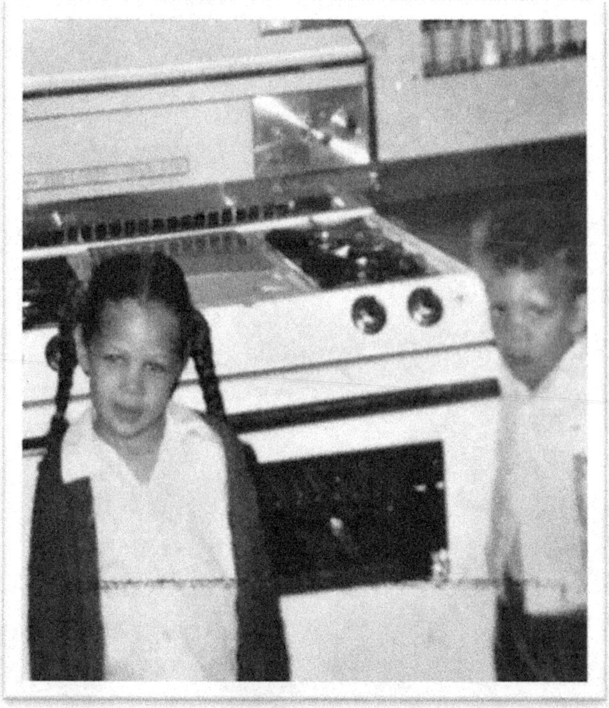

A QUICK POSE WITH MY BROTHER

LPG'S PROOF OF POSSIBILITY
LESSON 5: BRILLIANCE

My brother and I were latch key kids, because that was just the way it had to be. We had to make our family of three work reliably and efficiently, so to have a confidence in the utility of this, my father instilled in us a protocol that was to be followed under heavy threat of punishment. On Saturdays, thankfully there was relief, and we could all relax together for the good of the household order. Come Sunday mornings, we would sometimes go to church, but not always. To some extent we were heathens. We could not possibly have an ordinary lifestyle because my father was not a mother, and one was not in the house for a very long time until he married again. I suppose left to other devices we would have gone astray, but my father ruled with a look that could wither a thought of mischief before it connected from brain to transgression, and we unquestionably dared not go against his expectations. During these years, my father also held himself to a corresponding very disciplined protocol. He would be right on time at home when he got off work in the evening. His duties were to cook our dinner and go over our homework with thorough precision. Believe me, of all subjects, it was merciless to be corrected in math by my father. Math was a subject that came to him like magic. Not so for me. I would often leave the kitchen table where I did my homework in frantic tears, because he insisted that I had to pay attention and redo my problems until I understood what I was doing. Keep in mind he never insisted I got everything perfect—he emphasized that he wanted me to understand the thinking and processes behind the method. This was often harder than just following a formula, which in any math problem could eventually be done since there was always a finite right answer. Yet basically finding the right answer was never his ultimate goal. To push me forward, he would often say that I was much smarter than the problem in front of me, but until I believed it, I could not solve it. This was the beauty of how my father taught us to approach anything. He had several personal theorems about problem solving, and I specifically remember the virtuosity of one of them in particular.

We had a big white-topped kitchen table, where my books could spread out, with room enough to share manageable homework space with my brother. This setup was great because we could talk across the table, sharing our thinking regardless of the circumstance that we were separated by one class grade. My brother would typically make fun of me when I was stumped and frustrated, and soon our homework time degraded completely into badgering, until we checked the clock and assessed that our father would be home soon. We needed to finish our homework before dinner. Once dinner was finished and cleaned up, our father would check our work. One evening when I was about twelve, I became completely despondent over the subject of slope and line intercepts. They made absolutely no sense to me, and I could not fathom them conceptually or visually. So, while I feared leaving this part of my homework blank and a sure trigger for discussion with my father, I could no longer endure the headachy feeling that was slowly coming on. I was intense about my schoolwork and truly hated to be defeated. Timidly, I showed my work, or rather the deficiency of it, to my father that evening. I braced myself for his insistence to think harder. Instead he surprised the heck out of me!

"Well, I see that you need another way to think about this subject. So, let me give you a different approach. Matter of fact, I think I will advance you ahead of your class!" "Okay…" I challenged, and sat back in my chair with crossed arms, intrigued by what he would offer next.

"I see that it's time for you to understand LPG's Theory of Possibility!" Now, my father although a details-oriented guy, was exceptionally funny, so I relaxed. The letters LPG were his initials, which lead me to quickly infer that he had created and branded this idea already in his mind just for me. "Do I have to memorize it, Dad?" I did not really want to engage in complicated work, however. "No, no, just follow me, and try to understand what I am showing you. You should be able to get it after this. Pay attention."

He sat down and proceeded to ask me to rip out a blank page from my notebook because he needed to draw a diagram. "No, Dad, no diagrams please. This is hard enough," I insisted as I passed the paper to him. He also wanted four colored pencils. Oh no, I dreaded this becoming highly complex…

"Here, look at this," he indicated to the blank page. Watch, I am going to draw an x and y axis and divide the diagram into quadrants. You already know how to mark x and y, but instead of x and y, I want you to label the axes as "Freedom", where x would be, and "Opportunity" where y would go." Hmmm, I thought to myself. At this point we had the following:

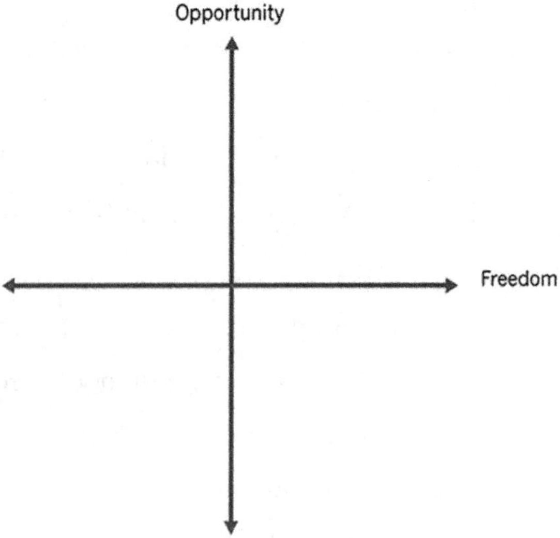

"Next, you will need to appropriate the value direction of each axis, so you should place the positive and negative indicators accordingly as well." That was easily done, no problem. So far, so good. "In addition, before we proceed you need to complete the structure of the graph by indicating the relative value of each quadrant, per the set of points that will best describe each quadrant. For example, negative x's and y's describe the quadrant with all negative values, and positive x's and ys' describe the quadrant with all positive values." Of course, I knew this already. He then added, "We will label them "I through IV." The chart now looked like this:

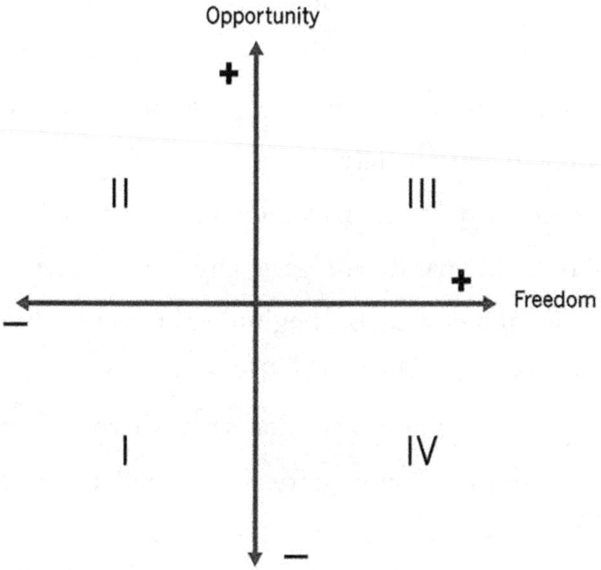

"...Okay, now I really do not understand what we are doing, or where you are going with this," I interjected. "Of course you don't," he said. "But now we are going to get crafty. We are not finished yet. Pay attention." "Yes, sir."

"Here is the essence of your lesson... We have drawn a chart where the values on this chart are critical in a context of "Oppression" versus "Possibility," meaning that we are creating a case where we can speak of Oppression or Possibility as tendencies you could designate on this chart. But before we can do that, we have one more thing to do so that any point on this graph is understood relative to another. The quadrants should be named to give any set of points a regional meaning. So, beginning in quadrant one, you can see that both the x's and y's have negative values. Consider that there is little Freedom or Opportunity, so we will name any point in this region as "Slaves." Moving clockwise, in the quadrant where x is still negative, but y is becoming positive, you can see we can now begin to identify some growing value of Opportunity but little Freedom. Well, we will label this quadrant region "Activists." Next, in quadrant III, where we find both x and y are positive, such that both Freedom and Opportunity can grow infinitely, we will call these points "Citizens." And then my father paused thoughtfully. "Now, for this last quadrant, where x can be greatly positive, but y can shift negatively, as if there could be great Freedom but Opportunity is squandered…we will call these points "Fools." With this, our chart was coming alive:

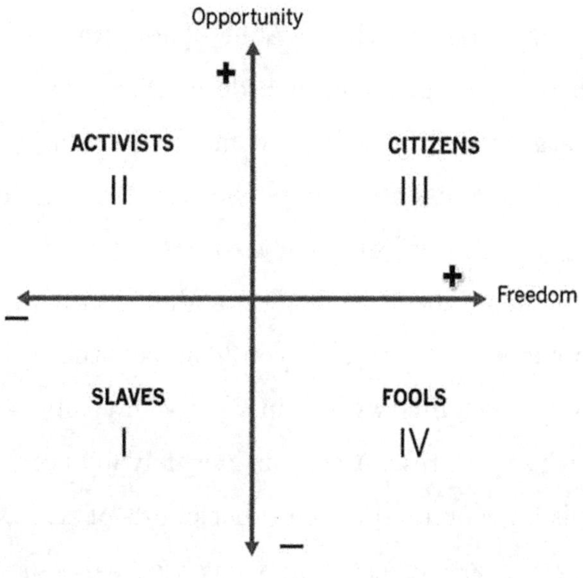

"Now, we can get down to business," my father said with a sly smile. "Right in front of you is a history lesson. I am going to pick a point on this graph that might represent the beginnings of freedom movements for Black people who were once enslaved. Thus, a point could be placed on the chart where it would signify no Freedom, although the hope of Opportunity, right on the cusp of the axis--as in a timeframe when your ancestors risked their lives to learn to read. In contrast, I am also going to choose a second point of importance, which could denote that while there were gains in Freedom, there was still marginalized Opportunity, much like what your parents, aunts and uncles chose to fight against. Again, as if right on a cusp, this point could represent the beginning of the Civil Rights movement. Hence, if you connect these two extreme points with a line, you can easily see a path of progress. Also, consider that any point on this line could represent other points of activism, but we are focused on what we will call the tipping points, for the sake of our conversation. This chart looked like the following:

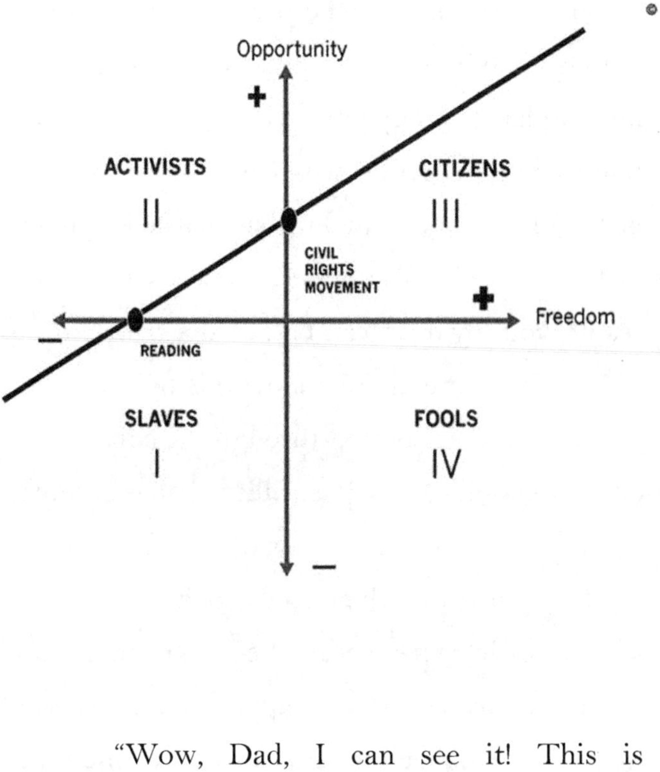

"Wow, Dad, I can see it! This is amazing!" "Yes, true. So, let's go on. We are not finished yet. Let's move over to what is happening in quadrant III, where there is unlimited Freedom and unlimited Opportunity. But pause for a minute and think about how your great-grandparents were slaves as in quadrant I, and how your grandparents survived Jim Crow as in quadrant II. Also recognize that moving through quadrants can be tireless! Finally, there are also acts that can push past a tipping point into a quadrant. Say your mother and I were on that tipping point in II with Civil Rights, but, the births of you and your brother marked changes in both Opportunity and Freedom, where as a result, you my dear, can be called a true Citizen of III! Look here, if you follow this line, you can technically keep soaring through the constraints of Oppression into a Possibility that is infinite, right? Do you see it?" I saw it!

"Stay with me, then. Let's look at that line again a little more closely. See, you can clearly move forward, dependent upon the choices you make. The farther forward you go on this line, the better off you are. Your choices represent the future, your "Possibility line"—which is nothing more than the tradeoffs you make between your Opportunities versus your Freedom. The goal of Possibility would be to gain more Opportunity and more Freedom. Oppression, a different state, occurs in just the opposite way. Do you see that?"

I saw it.

I was smiling hugely. And then I had a few questions. "Dad, what if my Possibility line is different than yours? Can that happen? What if instead of Civil Rights stuff, there might be another point that determined where my Possibility line intersected my Opportunity axis? You know what I mean?

"Exactly!!!" It was my father's turn to be excited now. I was happy too, because I was now in synch with him. "Exactly!" he repeated. "Do you know what causes that key difference? That factor is called Time! Time can change relevancy. So, we can push even further with this. We can make the chart look like 3D…Here you go:"

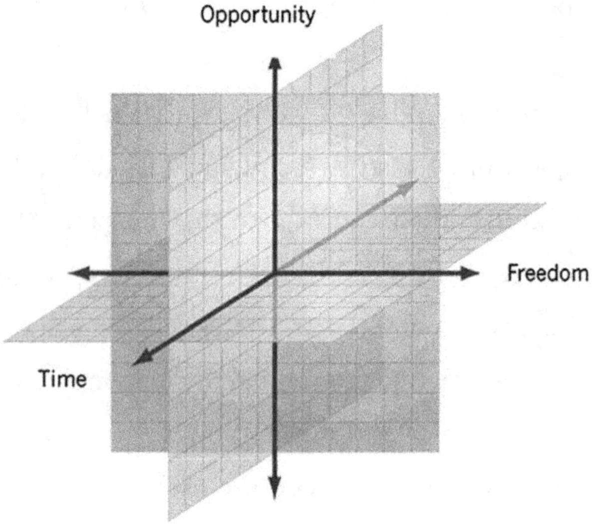

"So… if you understand all of this, you now also understand what the term "slope" means, what the terms "x and y intercepts" mean, and what causes different shifts to occur on a graph. Because you are what…?" And to this I knew to answer, "…I am smarter than the problem in front of me!" "That's right!" my father beamed. "Most excellently, you have also just demonstrated to yourself something that the great writer James Baldwin once wrote, "...Despite a history you did not deserve, you do not have to be defined by it!" Anything is Possible for you—the "LPG theory" is real--we just proved it!"

I did not need a moment like this to know how lucky I was to have a brilliant father who enjoyed coaxing genius out of his children. Of course, I went back to school the next day and excelled in my homework and classroom discussions. I soon became bolder about approaching complexity and enjoyed searching for interrelationships and patterns. To be honest, I preciously kept these pictures in my head all throughout college, and my career. "LPG's Proof of Possibility" was an undeniable breakthrough, treasured as an "Affirmation proof" for me. In this process, my father went to an extreme effort to prove the validity of Black generational progress in a manner that I could discern and comprehend easily. His goal was that with an entrenched understanding, coupled tightly with an ingrained anchoring that Possibility was expected of me, I could unshakably determine my own trajectory to affect change. He succeeded, as did I.

HOPSCOTCH
LESSON 6: AWARENESS

The cape was an over-the-top accessory, but seemed befitting for my Uncle Vic who, although was a prominent minister and public figure in San Francisco, was more importantly going to be the newest family connection that I would have to get used to--since he was to be the presiding minister at my father and stepmother's wedding. I had never seen anything like him before because neither my father, my brother, nor I, attended churches of the Baptist faith, and in particular, those that were on the radio each Sunday like his was. But the cape, and all that came with it, was to usher in my teenage and young adult years, during which I would be explicitly pressured to choose a side of the color line to be on, and to learn the folly or consequences of doing so.

My brother and I observed our brand-new uncle's arrival into the house from our posts on the balcony over the front door. We smirked surreptitiously at each other because not only was this "cape effect" flamboyantly new to our familial consciousness, we wondered how our father was going to take it all in as well. We were expected downstairs immediately for dinner, so we bounded down the staircase and quite politely introduced ourselves. Our stepmom-to-be was a wonderful cook and had set the table bountifully. With eager swiftness, I hungrily reached for a biscuit from the breadbasket after our dinner prayer, when, "And what scripture will you offer for the meal this evening?" rumbled from across the table. Alerted, I quickly took my hand back. The question had been directed to my brother who was sitting next to me, as was our habit. I looked at my father with an "Is he kidding?" kind of exasperation, and then to my brother with a "Fake it the best you can!" telepathic admonition. I knew for certain my brother could not effortlessly recall any profound Bible verse extemporaneously as was requested. This pomp and circumstance had never been a requirement to eat a meal at our house. I glanced across the table at my Uncle Vic and saw he had the dourest expression on his face that I had ever witnessed. I suppose my brother noticed the same, because he reverently bowed his head and gravely, simply, replied, "Jesus!" That did it! We broke into waves of hysterical laughter and had to be excused from the table. Resigned, my father advised we go back upstairs to our bedroom lairs, in order that dinner could be normally resumed, and the serious business of ceremony preparation discussed. It was the only thing that could be done because there was no way to salvage our derelict behavior. We were, who we were. Non-Baptist infidels.

But the matter at hand was a large one for the two of us as we pragmatically considered our father's impending marriage. We had never been asked before to conform our points of view to accommodate a belief system outside of the framework of the rainbow world we understood. We now had to think about how we could, and would, navigate courteous relationships with our new family and their mono-cultural perspectives, in a most heightened way. It would be the task of our stepmother to wisely and safely lead us through that dimmed tunnel. Only thirteen years older than I, she radiated a new layer in the spectrum of our future lives. As vibrant and lovely as a movie star, she was an independent, ultra-stylish, fun-loving, cool, urbanite. She had no problem understanding my outlier spirit. She encouraged my artistic self-expression whether it would be in designing houses or clothes, jewelry making or writing, and was a great partner alongside me in many of those endeavors. At the same time, she realized the enigma of my personality as being one that was also rooted deeply in a place where Black was not an absolute all of the time. But it would be Black experiences, those introduced to me by my stepmother, which considerably shaped my confidence and self-esteem in bold measure. I believe this is the reason God sent her to love my brother and me, so that we could effectively arm ourselves for the real world outside of my father's house. It may be the case that I will never agree with how society defines race and place, but it is with certainty during those years that I became aware of how it is that I am easily ascribed with an abundance of Blackness, and my Whiteness is just as easily dismissed. In these days, I was shown how to anticipate and maneuver through the obsequious ways in which others would self-righteously put me in the racial box they most easily understood.

While my mother and father so lovingly bestowed upon me the audacious characteristics of impassioned, visionary and independent thinking, my stepmom poured into me a maturing, honest, thoughtful realization that Black beauty is quite a devastating power. Watching and imitating her, I learned to move nimbly and proudly with this footing. Whereas, she conceded I was certainly a daughter who tempestuously defied pedestrian racial and cultural restriction, she just as readily knew that the world would never allow me that freedom. Being the remarkable Black woman she was, she shared tactics for rising above those social expectations that might instigate limitations or become attributed to me as weaknesses. And as difficult as some of the lessons were to receive, especially when I learned them the hard way, she continued teaching, mentoring and encouraging me without fail. Thus, under the glorious tutelage of my gutsy stepmother, I embraced a visage of beauty and fashion that freely and enthusiastically celebrated my curly hair, had an infatuation for big hoop earrings and a penchant for chic colorful ethnic attire that could be authentically worn. Humorously, these new expansions of cultural appetites were also combined with a susceptibility for heirloom pearls and platinum brooches, alligator purses and cashmere sweater sets. All of them were fun for me.

I soon realized that my mother, too, was appreciative and eternally grateful. Surprisingly, she and my stepmother forged an unusual alliance by befriending each other as co-parents. They made quite a pair, one mother White, one mother Black. One, hands-on and involved in our daily living. One, present daily even from afar. I laugh nostalgically about how much in step they were on several big occasions, such as when they coordinated their spring white linen tailored suits for my college graduation, both of them showing up in regal purple silk blouses, or, the way they commanded the kitchen cooking together for my father's seventieth birthday party. Their most favorite thing to do was to introduce themselves to our friends as our "Mothers." My brother and I would never clarify. I reluctantly explain the "how" of it even now, finding it to be redundant, since it seems important only that I have loved my experiences without such hackneyed distinctions. However, what I most admirably note is that these two devoted women believed and affirmed as on one accord, that I did truly possess those ideal talents to aptly succeed in the professions and disciplines that indifferently once excluded them.

My mother never received a grade lower than an "A" in her life and had earned a full tuition scholarship to the University of Notre Dame, with aspirations to become an engineer. But painfully, she was dissuaded by my grandfather and forced to become a nurse instead, as her mother had done. My stepmother had to leave college early to independently support herself, and never gained reassurance or the financial ability to return. She was extremely creative and entrepreneurial, yet she could not actualize her long-held dream of owning a business due to family pressures to earn a living in the traditional role of secretary. Co-mothering allowed shared vicarious ambitions, accolades, achievements and accomplishments on many fronts. Together, we three earned my degrees and promotions. My stepmother typed every single college paper, implacably earning my Bachelor of Science in business administration with me. My mother counseled me throughout my ascending corporate management career, having held several administrative management positions herself, knowing that glass ceilings were real and waiting. They laughingly called themselves the "Peanut Gallery." Anytime I came to them for questions and advice, they abetted me to stand stronger, taller, and to evolve consummately.

My Mothers did not ask me to choose a side between them, or to choose a racial preference because of them. When situations on each side of the color line spat me out as if I did not belong, which happened on several precarious occasions, my Mothers insisted I continue to obdurately and tenaciously forge my path regardless. Call it what you will, but I took their advice and learned to play hopscotch across lines, not tarrying too long on any one side perilously, yet always with a focused and constant forward motion toward some last played square. But eventually, I did choose. I made the same choice they both had made, for love. My preference was ordained by marriage to a Black man, then consecrated again in motherhood, to Black sons. With an undiluted cogency, our bonds as women and family came full-circle. My Mothers understood my choice and why I felt intensely compelled to make it. They respected I did so of my own volition, and they admired my earnestness—with one caveat.

My Mothers required my promise to them that I would bring my "full and present self" to bear in decision-making, whether on the Black or White side of the line. The chatter from the Peanut Gallery was unyielding about my remaining true to an ineradicable awareness of my gifted potential and value, underscoring that it never be diminished by race or gender, or stolen by bigotry, or, by any man. Without surprise to them, I have ardently kept that intentional and magnificent pledge. Gratifyingly, because of them, I have emerged as that sentient woman they destined me to one day be.

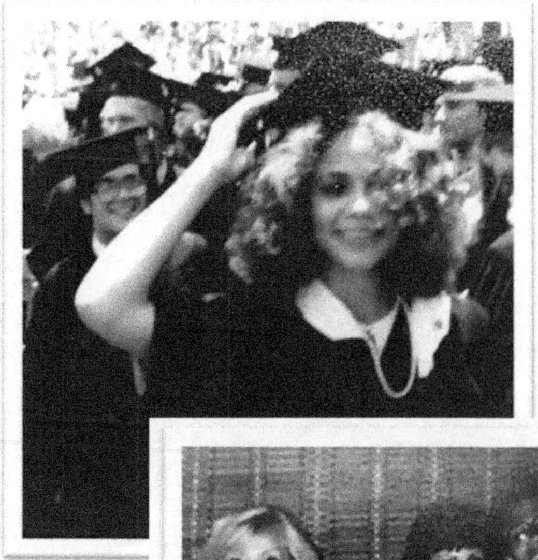

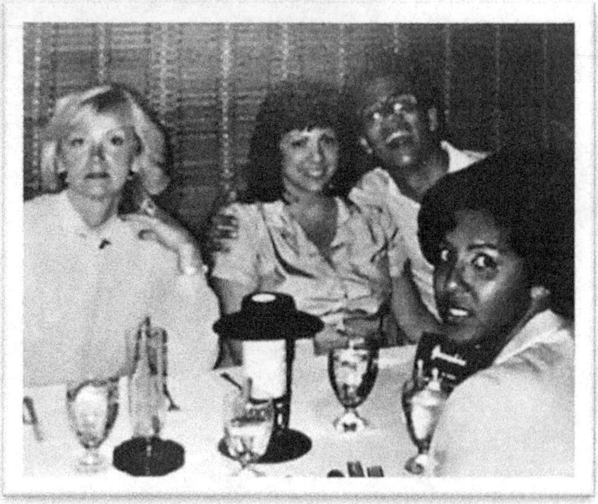

GRADUATION FROM COLLEGE —
I COULDN'T HAVE DONE IT WITHOUT MY MOTHERS!

SOUTHERN DAUGHTER
LESSON 7: HONOR

"Oh Nelly," these irises are beautiful!" my Grandma Helen elatedly proclaimed to my Grandma Nell over their long-distance phone call. "Why, I'm going to send Sheli out to the garden right now to find a spot for them. I think they will be perfectly wonderful next to the rhododendron." Or, perhaps on another occasion, "Well merciful heavens, you are so welcome! Charlie and I thought you and Ward would like those Japanese pears. They are supposed to be the sweetest this time of year…Well, bye now, yes, we'll see you soon."

My grandmothers were constantly sharing their garden between them. One time it would be lamb's ears to plant and another time it would be pink peonies, a new color for one grandmother that the other didn't yet have. It was hard to know where anything essentially originated, but their gardens were utmost sources of pride and joy. My grandfathers too shared their bounty between them. My Granddaddy Ward would send something fresh from the summer vegetable garden, and in return, my Grandpa Charlie would send a new page of stamps from the post office because they were both keen collectors. That, and maybe a bottle of bourbon they both liked. My summers were full of sharing between the houses, just a Greyhound bus away. My brother and I could pack up suitcases and our bikes easily, and load them to the underside of the bus, take our tickets out, and ride between Abingdon and Bluefield like old pros. At our youngest, we were nine and ten, yet unafraid of traveling alone. At the end of the trip would be smiles of grandparents to receive us. In between would surely be green hills stretching along the highway bounded by old streams and rivers, grand dames of old Virginia farm estates, or perhaps jagged well-worn dirt paths leading to someone's trailer home. Wire fences marked off one patch of farmland or cow pasture from another. You could tell the time of day by the meeting of cows under trees, knowing that the heat of the midday sun would drive them to shade. Although there were several stops, the bus ride was never too long. We carried our packs of candy and food to eat, so we never had to get off. We knew how to exist in the adventure of our journey, careful not to argue or fight with each other--until we arrived and were freed into a grandfather's car.

But on this day, in an earliest morning, the Virginia sky hung around me in a too familiar embrace. I could close my eyes and see again the girl I had once been, racing across the tarmac into the waiting arms of my grandmother and grandfather, dark silhouettes engulfing a vibrant golden pillow of a child. Kisses and laughter and hugs were affirmations of my family connection, the essence of each homecoming. As the sun broke over the mountain ridge in the distance, I stood at the bridge of the hull door, my hair whipping in the gusts of the airplane tailwinds. Across the horizon of the tarmac this day was only a sea of White people, waving excitedly to cousins, sisters, brothers, husbands and wives. I was none of these. Each of my steps down the metal stairs from the plane's small front door rang out insurgently. My high-heels continued a haughty staccato down the long terminal hallway to the baggage claim area. "No, thank-you," I did not need a skycap today. "No, thank-you," I did not need assistance to find the rental car counter. I took off my dark glasses to thank the elderly gray gentleman who insistently offered his graciousness, and then let him per chance consider my deep yellow-green eyes framed by tanned, creamed skin and flowing waist length curls. An alarmed recognition, an old one, his stare instantly acknowledged that I was unmistakably a daughter of the South. I answered him with a disdainful silent reply, that I indeed was the truest daughter of a southern legacy. I collected my Louis Vuitton suitcase from the baggage treadmill and moved with heart sinking effort through the glass doors to the carport. Heads turned as I passed, my expensive perfume luxuriously wrapping around their curiosity. It was plainly apparent that I walked with the air of someone who had been through this small airport before, as if I were one of them. Purposefully, I exemplified the arrogant distance of more than a meager stranger. No, I would never desire in my wildest dreams to be one of them at all.

The closed car doors trapped the silence that emphasized much too loudly my press upon the accelerator. I was not disturbed by it, only I made a mental note that perhaps this car had seen more mountain driving than I was used to, and hence the wear and tear had to be negotiated. So be it. The mountains claimed me now. I knew the way home regardless of the car, or magic carpet chosen. I stole quickened glances all around me as I drove. The hills were dead with snow. The tree branches were black and splintered, lifeless, leafless. I had about three hours of mountain driving, and hopefully would get home before dark. I could taste the crispness in the air when I rolled the window down, and therefore knew that the afternoon would be falling soon. My father would meet me at the house, but that was not a totally comforting thought. I hoped my brother would be there as well, to help ensure that whatever turmoil awaited would somehow be muted. The radio clicked at the press of a button, and I lost myself in country songs I would be sure to never learn.

I breathed greedily. I needed the rich air of the Virginia highlands to coat my lungs and my memories, so that I could hold on for dear life, battling the grief beginning to seep through my skin. I felt the once protective air dissipating around me. This day, my grandmother would not be there peering through the screen door at the sound of my car in the driveway, to slowly manage a cane over the steps and the flower beds, or to command the light touch of a wrinkled hand to brush my mussed hair back from my face with a kiss of "Hello child, I love you." The stuttering motor announced my presence in the dark garage at twilight.

My luggage was easy to lift from the trunk because I packed only one suit. The rest of my clothes consisted of jeans and easy to pull on tee shirts, which took up very little space. I did not need my brother to help me with the bags, but I let him do so anyway because it filled the stretch of sadness between us. He walked in front of me, setting the example of strength I needed to cross through that threshold. Before I turned the hallway corner to take my things upstairs, I dared myself to glimpse into the bedroom that had been converted for my grandmother and saw that my father had already removed the bed. The room stood nearly bare, with the large square of where the bed and my grandmother had been, etched into the carpet. The space was still filled with an imprint of a tiny woman sleeping.

When I finished absently unpacking, I came downstairs and joined my father on the porch swing, quiet and thoughtful. His hugs were good, still offering the stability of Daddy to me. He easily made room so that I could sit and see the old church spires jutting up against the silence of the sky off in the distance of what was Main Street. He had grown so thin and had seemingly aged considerably in the year since I last visited. I sat and contemplated the larger spire, tall and gleaming over the old pecan trees even in the lateness of the evening, then next the smaller steeple of the weathered church just a few buildings down on the same street. From the time of my childhood, the meaning of the two Methodist churches in such proximity, on the same street, bewildered me. On Sundays, when I walked up the worn steps of the smaller plain church, I would swell with pride upon seeing the yellowed documents encased in glass near the door. I knew by heart just where my great-grandparents' signatures were that historically commemorated the building with the dedication of the church to allow worship for the freed slave. My great-grandparents had helped to build this church, and it was filled with descendants that fortified its sanctuary currently. Those same Sundays I also brusquely walked passed the large, fine mahogany doors of the other church, the White church, never crossing the doorstep, or wanting to peer in its windows. Although it was celebrated in the area for its beautiful stained-glass windows, it remained to me a relic, unapproachable. I knew my father had once swept floors there when he was younger, making small pocket change in high school. I would often imagine my father spitting into the dust on the sidewalk outside each time he closed and locked the doors for the night, before his short walk home. "Paying his respects", he told me.

My grandmother was buried in the integrated cemetery, next to my grandfather, the only other family I had in that ground. All the rest of my kin were buried up on the hill on the south side of town on Taylor's Hill, in the Black cemetery. There, four generations welcomed each other, celebrating a bloodline even in death. My grandfather had purchased the new plots in the 1970s, feeling somehow that his ability to even do so was important to our social progress, but as I looked around that afternoon, noting my mother as the exception, only Black faces stood in communion and shed their tears for my grandmother. I did not remain to see the casket lowered into the ground. I refused to see my grandmother like a package in a box, given over to the dirt. I thought about the chill of my leather gloves against my fingers, and decided it was time to leave this place. I would not be staying in Abingdon too long. I had come to say my words for my last grandmother, only to find that she had wanted a very simple service and did not want the mourning of her grandchildren to crowd her ascension into Heaven.

My parents were still alive, but I considered myself an orphan. All my grandparents had gone on to Glory, and I was left behind, alone without them. My dauntless grandparents had been my refuges, providing calm in the noises of my life. I was blessed because I had incredibly loving relationships with them all. The fact that each one of them created safe and loving places in their lives for my brother and me signified loudly, breaking through barriers of common people's social insensitivities. Just as I was embraced and adored on Kings Mountain in Abingdon, I was also unquestionably known as Charlie's and Helen's granddaughter, and devotedly taken about when I came to Bluefield. I knew many racially mixed children who grew up with me in San Francisco. Most of them only knew one side of their parents' families. Rarely did they know both, or were acknowledged by both, or experienced love as an inclusive family. I never knew that kind of emptiness, which is why my grandparents were my first real superheroes in disguise. However, it would not be a true statement to say that they did not see race as being problematic. In fact, each of them agonized when my parents married. If their first common bond was a necessity to protect and nurture their grandchildren, this paved the way for ties that became unbreakable. I grew into my adulthood knowing with an unwavering conviction that people could choose to love and respect each other despite artificial obstacles, race being one of those.

For all their supposed differences, my southern grandparents were very much the same. As a child, this caused me great consternation because even young, I could tell that few realized what I saw due to racial blindness. Sometimes I did feel like Alice on the other side of the looking glass. Further, I would puzzle often about which side of the glass was the right or wrong side, because I also knew not to trust what others wished me to believe, given what they would say accompanied by their reactions. I later created a logic that permeated my reflections, and I learned to reach through each side of the glass when I found I needed something of use. As simple examples of their similarities, both of my grandfathers were Masons and both of my grandmothers were Eastern Stars. All of my grandparents were Methodists. More deeply, their morality and social constructs were the same, believing that the most important possession one had was their integrity, and the most important gift one could give was their word. I grew up with books, mahogany, walnut, and cherry antiques, hand-laced linens, silver flatware and tea sets in the large dining rooms of both homes. Both of my grandmothers had beautiful flower gardens and cooked many of the same foods. They did needlepoint, embroidery, sewed, knitted and crocheted, and both commiserated on teaching me the same. My grandfathers both loved woodworking. They could make anything, and they could fix anything. The smoked the same brand of cigarettes, and both liked their bourbon. But certainly, as I got older, I did understand that despite the lack of significant variances between them, there were certainly the irrefutable signals when socially imposed racial inferiority caused distinction. My indomitable grandfathers both had sixth grade educations, but only one had the ability to create power without the drudgery of having to inflect "Yes sirs" or "Yes ma'ams."

My grandparents each had a proud attachment and reverence for the land they were from. Summers with them would be spent outdoors in fenceless backyards, picnicking on a lake, or adventuring in a state park. I grew up knowing their close friends and acquaintances alike, and spent many evenings on porch swings and patios listening to country politics before I went to bed. Their gentility doted upon me and embraced me. I never realized, until I graduated from college, the quiet manner in which my grandparents also made their accord with several relationships that socially left them. But I never knew those people.

Come the weekends, and every holiday, there was an accounting of everyone, either with phone calls, presents in the mail, shared church services or dinners in their homes. As my grandparents aged, the roles and responsibilities by which they watched over and cared for each other changed and shifted. My Grandma Helen was a severe diabetic, and she was the first to become frail. My Grandma Nell never got over losing her. My Grandpa Charlie often told me that my Granddaddy Ward was the smartest man he ever knew, and that he had lost a brother after his early death. Now, with the passing of my last grandmother at 92, and this finality of their chapters together, I felt like the last man standing.

After her funeral, the rest of my time was spent with family sifting through clothes, jewelry, estate information, desk drawers, contacting thrift shops, speaking with attorneys, acknowledging sympathy cards and flowers. Other family, cousins and friends, came to visit so that they too could hear the last echoes of my grandmother in the house before those faded. This part of the ritual was necessary, because it called forth a reunion of the family remaining and our living history. Our tribe was slowly declining in Abingdon. So many of the young, including myself, had been told to leave and not make a future there in order that our family could advance beyond the residues of slavery, sharecropping and Jim Crow. The collective aspiration was that we would chase equality in substantially more progressive and burgeoning opportunities. Yet, many of my aunts and uncles grew old and lonely without their young around them, and consequently we became somewhat lost from each other. My grandmother had dependably represented our only trusted and commanding link to the past because she knew how our family had come to the town, settled, married and thrived. She had always been the reservoir from which everyone came to drink. Grandmother could tell them how closely they were related to each other, as well as to those whom some of them still cleaned houses for, or tended the store for at the historic mill site. She knew the town lore, including those whispered truths which were silenced to establish orderly and peaceful existences south of the railroad tracks on the hill called Kings Mountain.

Kings Mountain could be seen directly from my bedroom window, a short walk away. Each of the families on Kings Mountain were related to me, and all of the Black families, with small exception lived there. My grandparents grew up there, but did not reside there, and famously lived on the north side of those tracks. My grandfather purchased a parcel in 1933 cheaply because it was in close proximity to the railroad. The other two families to follow suit were my great-grandfather and a cousin, and these acreages were all connected to form a contiguous square in what later became the historic part of town. This compound became known for its beautiful flowering landscapes and was a sort of landmark of community life imposed beyond the train track color line. It was also a landing place for Black dignitaries who would not be given courtesies otherwise in town, to include Justice Thurgood Marshall who was a guest there.

During my lifetime of summers, I could luxuriate under the willows, chestnut, pecan walnut, cherry, apple and magnolia trees that my grandfather planted. I could sink into blankets under showers of wisteria next to rose gardens bordered with queen anne's lace hydrangeas and peonies, with mowed grass lawns shaped by precisely trimmed boxwoods. My mornings began with homemade applesauce from the fallen apples of my grandfather's grafted five-apple tree. Sometimes the days would end with my special favorite of corn pudding, made from fresh corn I eagerly chose from the garden, or custard ice cream with sweet blackberries picked from trellised vines and hand churned in the afternoon.

Summers and Kings Mountain could not be separated for me. My life was connected to the houses I visited, and to all the people I would be re-introduced to each year. They were my blood and welcomed me always as their own, folding every sun-streaked ringlet of my hair into every lavender embrace. My history was mutually contextual, understood and forgiven. At the end of these summers, I would typically return home carrying a Park Belk hatbox with me on to the small plane that would soar loudly out of the mountain highlands. Its treasure, a homemade chocolate cake with chocolate icing, would be tied so carefully by one of my grandmothers. When I finally got to sit down at my table I could relish my connection to my homeland and to my family bite by bite, over the years sharing also with my husband and sons.

When I returned from my Grandmother Nell's funeral, I carried no hatbox. I was grieving so. I drove the rental car back to the airport, kept my dark glasses on, and quietly tipped up the narrow steps into the plane and buckled myself in. I would never again be anyone's beloved grandchild. Those bus rides of flower transports were long over. My guardian angels Nell, Helen, Ward and Charlie rest easy though, as I forever cherish the way they loved each other, and, loved me. I never fail to pay them the honor of remembering just whom I did belong to once upon a time. I ever remain a Southern Daughter.

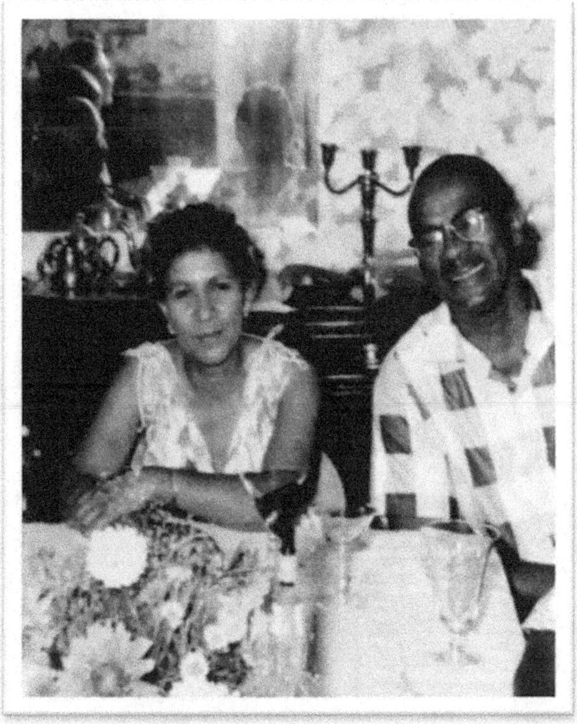

GRANDMA NELL AND GRANDDADDY WARD
ENTERTAINING AT HOME.

INTERLUDE:
GYPSY

Unmovable fates have timelessly chiseled my
spirit,
Edges invisible perhaps, but nonetheless
enduring.
Hence, I hearken to love
My family, more protectively;
My friends, more reservedly;
My intentions, more determinedly.
It's been said my temperament once beamed
with the Favor of Harmony,
Laughing, giving, amenable,
Before Reason pierced the Veil.
My sentiments are no longer loyal to an
unkempt History.
They are now Glorious Gypsies,
Fey Evangelists,
Inspired Nomads,
Seeking manifest sanctuary, awaiting discovery.
And I will surely, incontestably, find it.

SONGBIRD
LESSON 8: RESILIENCE

I am very lucky to have had several very different professional careers, but I started out like most do: knowing little about the real world, yet learning because of living through what I did not have the experience to anticipate. My first lifetime ago, I was a young gun in the summer of 1981. I remember on my very first day, I felt so triumphant in the pre-workday morning because I had safely, albeit timidly, guided my stick shift car into my office building parking lot, after breakfast threats from my brother refusing to drive me. He insisted vehemently that I should become independent of him and unafraid to drive myself. Well, I was independent no problem, but I did not know how to drive a stick shift, and therefore was indeed a bit afraid. I was a bit angry too, because I had purchased the car based upon promises from him to teach me to drive it—but I had to put that behind me in sisterly apartment co-tenant fashion, so I swallowed several prideful words with my toast and coffee. With intense focus and determination, I got into the car, and pointed it in the right direction. "It" was a present from my grandfather for graduation. Sleek, sporty, both the car and me! I successfully downshifted over the railroad tracks at the first major intersection, and later, held the clutch while stopping on a hill. I felt a little better with each mile. Because I had been so nervous about my morning, I arrived early. Next on my agenda was to walk through those lobby doors and begin earning my first paycheck!

I worked earnestly and avidly for ABC, a premier computer corporation, from 1981 to 1996. Fresh faced at twenty-one, I was hungry and eager, with brilliance in my back pocket and a fervent work ethic as my inheritance. Over the course of nearly fifteen years I held, and was speedily promoted through, coveted positions titled Marketing Trainee, Systems Engineer, Marketing Representative, Marketing Training

Instructor, Industry Field Advisor, Marketing Manager, and eminently Senior Management Consultant. Highlights of my career included progressing through it at a rapid rate, wherein I achieved top sales awards each year and the bonuses to accompany them. I earned my first one hundred thousand dollars by the time I was twenty-eight, when at that time, I became one of the youngest Marketing Managers in the company. I traveled the world. I earned my MBA, and the company paid for it. I could live the life my family wished for me. Along the way, I also married and birthed two sons. The mesh of my professional and personal life was a crazy one. I would stake a multi-million-dollar computer deal during the day, and then cook a full meal for my family in the evening. I would casually take a conference call from home with an executive vice president during my six-week maternity leave, while feeding a bottle to my newborn son in my arms. Across several time zones when I attended business conferences or lived countries away on assignment, I would routinely check over my son's homework via the fax machine in my hotel room. I had ambitions of being the first corporate executive in my family, and I could see the possibilities unfolding. The spin of my world was one of the most impressive that anyone who knew me had seen. The pace was so fast it appeared that my life circumstances as a wife, a mother, a woman, a professional, were perhaps extreme, but could possibly be a new normal. I was exuberant and exhausted at the same time in the blur of it all. Yet, the world careened to a tumultuous halt the day the graceless main course of Racism was served to me on a most bitter plate. I got dizzy, sick, and I needed to quickly trust my survival instincts.

Others reading this should take care to remember that I am not telling their story, and that this remembrance is merely a small glimpse into the full telling of mine.

Growing up listening to my father's many conversations at the end of his day, I vicariously learned the subtle, extremely likely, creep of on-the-job racism. I heard and observed how it insidiously vaporized into political correctness over the course of the nineteen seventies, eighties and nineties, and consequently saw what forty years of desensitization in corporate professional environments could do. Just two generations prior, my family would move from subsisting in rural small-town desolation to brimming with an urbanely influenced sophisticated respectability, so my kaleidoscope was all the pretty designs of the middle class. I turned and twisted the end of that long generational scope and saw in the shadows behind the designs the treacheries of my father's career as a Black professional. Thus, as I began to advance in my own corporate career, I should have been able to sense an end run using my honed recognizance. But I never saw it because I was distracted with the pace of my life, and I was tackled to the ground with no mercy.

...One of the things I most loved to do each time I relocated my desk, or settled into a new promotion, was to prominently arrange my family pictures. No matter the state or city, I would invariably get that benign question, "Who are these people?" Depending on the tone, it was easy to detect the curious versus the rude. From the start, I accepted the role of being the oddity in the office. While it did not ever diminish my self-confidence, the commonness of my White co-workers often would surprise me, and I could depend on them to always appear bewildered by whomever the individuals could possibly be. In contrast, I was never left to wonder why my Black peers and associates never asked, and we would often trade sincere and humorous comments back and forth in the office about the handsomeness of each other's families, and about who was doing what, or how much the little ones were growing.

On many occasions, my corporate world would push my personal buttons. When I was first a Trainee, my curriculum encompassed nearly two years of corporate education. I would live in a company compound with six other roommates, and attend class for eight hours a day, six weeks at a time. First thing each morning, we would sit bleary eyed at our desks subjected to a daily motivational video. The topics of these videos would vary, such that I learned about the adventures and challenges of mountain climbing, Indy car racing, yachting, football coaching, anything that presented daunting personal sacrifices and tests of the human condition to persist, with the ultimate achievement of winning. At the end of these videos, the room would go black, the instructor would turn up the lights and the class would have group discussion about the applicability of these new ideals. However, one day, I had a question: "Couldn't ABC find a video that depicted an African American also striving towards a goal—and winning?" My classes had never been shown one, and I struggled with the messaging I received. What was I to personally take from being shown each day, every day, that the only folk who could climb a mountain, race a car, steer a boat across the sea, meet a challenge, were so not like me? ...My request was never fulfilled. I supposed because we were in the pre-Michael

Jordan days that this was the reason we never even saw a basketball video.

During this time, I made the acquaintances of several African American instructors. They would provide my first introductions to unspoken lessons regarding climbing the corporate ladder. Becoming a Marketing Training Instructor was a job with a certain caché in the company. It meant that you were successful in the field, and had overachieved to the point that your skills and wisdom would be valuable exemplars to others. At that time, ABC was a company that only promoted from within, so the Instructor was a new trainee's first glimpse at Valhalla. As nice to me as these Black instructors were, they also taught me the strategic necessity of leaving much of my Black self at home. I respectfully appreciated them for unveiling those first warnings about how to align a professional life in a different parallel universe in order to remain sane, and sense making.

My training days were exercises of personal constraint, as well as intense lessons about computers, programming, selling, competing and of course, winning. Although we were few relative to the entire cohort, collectively and subversively, my Black classmates would rebel on occasion. One day for example, we had a difficult programming lab assignment. The objective was to utilize a specific proprietary programming language command to condition logic sequences to "chain" statements together that would produce a specific result. The lab would be over six hours long and was held after class. Late into that evening we worked in our group, separate from the other groups simply because it was rare for the others to willingly include a Black classmate. We were still unsuccessful at midnight. Finally, beyond the point of exhaustion and dinner hunger, a rising voice first soft and low, then louder, then with joined chorus, floated a rendition of "Chain of Fools" throughout the data center. Laughing, we made it through the night after all, and our group passed the exam with high lab marks by dawn.

The day I was promoted to Marketing Manager, I received calls from all over the country. I was the first of my African American peers whom I trained with to capture this brass ring. My friends were very proud of me, yet with every hug and congratulatory accolade, they would caution, "Just be careful!" On the other hand, when I found them for lunch or drinks after work, their congratulatory joviality was raucous. They knew that ABC did not think we had gotten the "joke." They retorted that clients would never see me coming. What was acknowledged by my friends, and by me, was that I was probably the least threatening looking Black person the company would dare put in front of a Fortune 500 account. The ascendancy of the "fair skinned Negro" was so shopworn, but true. I smelled the power of it sweetly, as back then I had nothing to lose.

The first thing I did was to redecorate my office. I took down the framed fruit and the English hunting pictures and put up Ernie Barnes prints. Again, my family pictures were on full display, which by this time also included my children. When I would be introduced to new executives and the discussion rambled to pulling out wallet pictures, I would be right there with them pulling out mine too. I was young, successful and brash. You either loved me, or you didn't. But if you worked for me, and helped make me successful, then you liked me a lot. I would boldly hold court in our branch office with just a little bit of flavor. Perhaps there would be the lilting volume of Hip-Hop music during the branch meetings I ran, or perhaps the branch skit would be performed to the tune of Kool Moe Dee's "Wild Wild West" to mesh with the cowboy and western theme. Once, because I had to host a branch kick-off meeting in Park City, Utah, and because the meeting was held on Martin Luther King, Jr.'s birthday and obligated the presence of all the African American employees—before it was a national holiday--I accommodated my colleagues with a fully rehearsed and choreographed marketing unit parody of MC Hammer's "U Can't Touch This."

It was hilariously entertaining and enjoyed by all, and I still made my point.

It is also inanely true that on a particular day, one of my co-workers asked me how I seemed to know every single Black person that worked in my building, noting the greetings I shared on the elevator during the many start and stops. I worked on the twenty-first floor. Face it, during these times, corporate African Americans needed to be covert. Although this was necessary, it also was fraught with undue pressure. Simple things would invariably spill over to be negotiated in my personal life. My husband never wanted my peer managers to come over to our house and see how we lived (just like they did); he was always warning me about wearing my mink coats in the winter on assignment (I would have to travel to New York or Chicago); I should not have driven a vice president to my accounts in my car (a Porsche). My husband's argument throughout these many scenarios, was that it was dangerous for me to look "too successful" or rather "as successful as them." He cautioned me about the predilection of my behavior. It was always a hard pill for me to swallow, and yet not heeding these warnings would ultimately lead me to end my corporate career.

I returned to Atlanta for an assignment as part of a project team in the newly formed ABC Consulting Group. By this time, after fourteen years, I had seen, heard and endured many quirky race-based situations. Yet regardless of the constancy of those, that day I squarely faced my breaking point. In this situation, there was a meeting with a client executive who apparently did not realize (or give a damn) that I was the African American member of the project consulting team. I believe he chose not to "see" me. Yes, and what can so easily happen when we are not "seen" happened. He made an abashedly defamatory remark about the consumer habits of Blacks with regard to his company's propensity to offer fast food products in Black urban markets, where they were making a great deal of money. We were auditing and reengineering site operations, to increase menu efficiencies and profit margins. He commented sarcastically about his reasoning of why quality blend coffee did not need to be served on the morning breakfast food menu that was being redesigned. "You know (wink, wink), those people won't know what they are drinking anyway, so we really don't need to offer it" ...I gulped—I was drinking my own cup of coffee at the moment of that remark. When I finished swallowing, I told him directly that he was wrong, and I assured him that if the coffee were any good, then WE'd surely drink it! I then excused myself from the project meeting and from the room, saying that I needed to get a refill of my delicious morning coffee. At lunchtime, I was called to the practice leader's office and asked to leave the project—because it was collectively perceived that my remarks were upsetting, unprofessional and offensive. You did not have to ask me twice. I took my mink-coat-wearing, husband-is-doctor, Armani-suited-ass right out of the front door!

The harshness of that one situation was not the reason in total that caused me to leave the company, and then to sue them. I had handled ignorance before, but for the first time in my career, my colleague who was the practice leader, did not respect me enough to pivot and reprimand the client as being out of bounds. It shocked and surprised me because "Respect for the Individual" was a primary tenet of the company at that time. The prevailing opinion by my all White ABC teammates was that I had overreacted. The project was, after all, a multimillion-dollar project, so my comments put the relationship at risk. Ironically, all the videos that I had been made to watch came back upon me like a ton of bricks. I realized in that moment, that they did have their application after all. Although I never saw an African American in any of them, the implicit messaging was that actually, I did have to scale mountains—higher, race in heated contests—faster, meet any challenge—with more agility. And while in the videos there were several implied incentives for diligence and perseverance, my personal footraces toward acclaim were going to have to be more obscured and subservient. In fact, I distinctly reflected upon how my Black colleagues were selected for competition differently from the very start. It was interesting to me that every single African American person I trained or worked with received their degrees in the sciences, math, business, or engineering. We held top tiered grade point averages. On the other hand, I worked with more than my share of non-African American trainees with liberal arts degrees and lesser academic profiles…go figure. Additionally, the better income opportunities were associated through the ranks of sales and marketing, but it was often difficult for African Americans to be equitably considered for these competitively lucrative territories, or to last long in them if placed. Thus, few African Americans were proportionately represented in the sales force, and fewer still in the sales management ranks. Where you would find us would typically be in technical support, product training, or in many of the jobs that remained behind the scenes instead of as the lead in front of an important client. As one of the few African Americans to hold such client facing positions corporate-wide, I also knew I was certainly not the only competent person worth the consideration. But I was now faced with a level of disrespect which was becoming a false narrative used to question and quell my leadership authority and flatten my expert input into invisibility. I had always and only been a top performer on record, so now with a situation where others were approved to take credit for my work and research in order to mollify a client, combined with my having endured one too many harassment situations that included sexual innuendo from older male colleagues and superiors, I decided to act. My husband became my backbone in bringing the case forward, and I needed one when I arrived at the opposing law office to face sixteen blue-suited White male lawyers seated around a grand oblong walnut conference table, placed to intimidate me along with inane questioning throughout a seven-hour deposition. It easily became apparent I was not crazy, but their strategy was to bankrupt me with escalating expenses so that crazy or not, I would walk away. In the end, after a year of building a case which included expert witnesses, while I did not win in court due to being only one voice and not able to challenge as a class action suit, being too far ahead of my time, much did change in the corporate setting. The company did find in their own investigation that my allegations were strongly substantiated. They offered me my position back and an apology. For another thing, a Black employee group was formally initiated and supported. Diversity forums and meetings would now be encouraged and engaged. I was very proud to have played a large part in ushering in those changes…yet, the company had lost its luster for me because I had lost my trust in its tenets. I was not bitter. The journey surprisingly strengthened me and revealed I could do better. I left officially in 1996, excitedly started my own business with my husband, and together we achieved revenues of over a million within two years. I have never looked back, nor been wistful of what might have been because my newfound autonomy put my expertise right up front and center, and my income at presidential levels. Interestingly, the lead internal investigators of my case eventually both became senior vice presidents of corporate diversity prior to their retirements, and were notably lauded and admired throughout the industry for their work. I say they had a great test case.

In hindsight, I think it is best to grapple with convincing others about the tricks, rather than the truths of racism, as its very essence lies in things not easily discerned or reenacted—even with evidence. Believing that racism is about what can be made obvious to the mainstream is to be exhaustingly maneuvered into circular arguments that attempt to absolve the perpetrator(s). To also allow others to believe that racism is simply about color, when it is fundamentally about destroying human value because of race, is also a grave error often overlooked. I am a contrarian. I do not believe the insufferable task to un-teach racism is for Black professionals to lead alone. What I do believe, is, that the cockroach-like, generational obstinacy, and terminal malevolence of racism must be a shared acknowledgement as the starting point of any real conversation about eliminating it. Without this kind of foundational articulation, comfortable or not, positive change will not be sustainable, and it cannot be trusted.

While Jim Crow has ostensibly passed into history, the current quandary begs how to move beyond impositions of Jim Canary. Racism continues to expand and flourish, marking indelible boundaries in endless permutations, like mental fences dotted across the brain. Whether barbed-wired or another anguishing barrier, somehow these must be gotten over, under, around and through. It will take adroit strategy and high gamesmanship to scale these fences grandly. Personally, I believe there is nothing more exhilarating than winning contests for deserved equitable freedoms—challenged not as canary birds fleeing from a cage--but as a people able to race, climb, leap, and conquer. I imagined that once, in a video.

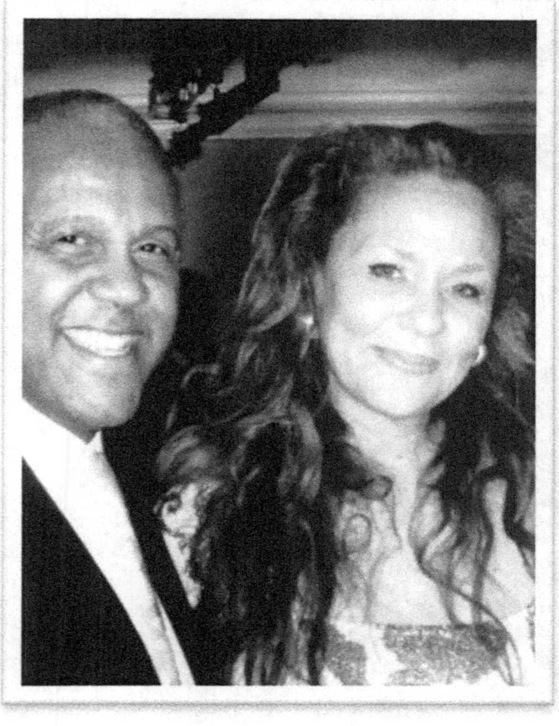

MY HUSBAND AND I,
REMARKABLE IN BUSINESS, LIFE AND
LOVE.

UNCHAINED MELODY
LESSON 9: RESOLVE

I have two very distinct memories of my eldest child as a slave. The first is from when he was in fifth grade, in a school play for a Black History presentation at his phenomenal predominately African American Montessori school. He and his classmates were up on the stage, on the plantation, in a field, picking cotton. He was four-and-a-half feet tall, dressed in old faded blue jeans and a washed-out and patched jeans shirt with the buttons mismatched. On his little head was an old weathered straw hat that I wore when I gardened. He stood on the stage barefoot with his friends as they recanted the misfortunes of life in the fields. It was heartbreakingly comical, but they were speaking of the injustices of slavery from their young perspectives and had written the play about it. My son was the fairest-skinned slave up there, obviously before he would have been sent out to those fields to suffer greatly in the sun. No matter, he was singing loudly, wiping his brow with an old dirty kerchief, a member of a happy chorus in bondage. Singing about picking cotton, toting a burlap sack. I took a picture of the little fifth grade slaves, all looking their slave best. When they saw this picture later in a class photo album, they laughed hysterically at themselves because they felt they looked ridiculously out of touch with their reality.

The second recollection of my son as a slave is centered upon his struggle and frustration to answer an essay question posed to him in an application to an elite private middle school. The question asked was, “If You Could Change an Historical Event, Which One Would That Be and Why?” He was thoughtful for some time, and then began to write eagerly on a scratch notepad before he would commit his words to the permanence of the application. This was his answer verbatim:

"If I could change an historical event, I would change the way Black people have been treated in this country. Black people have been known as a people that are not as intelligent as White people. I would change this thinking by going back in time before slavery. I would warn the African tribes that people from another land are coming to kidnap them. I would give them directions to Asia, so they could stay there for a while.

I would change these things because Black people today are treated unfairly. We are often brought down many times simply by a person saying we do not have enough qualifications to do a job. I know this opinion is not always true because everyone in my family studied and worked very hard to do well.

The impact my actions would have on the future would be that any Black person could be more successful because of their achievements. Everyone in the world would know about our accomplishments and inventions in history, than what is known today. My beliefs are that everyone should be treated fairly and given an opportunity to achieve their goals." …

My son does not know that I have saved this piece of scratch paper after all of these years, and that I hold his answer so preciously. After I read it that first time, I could neither suggest that he add any further thought, nor delete any. I too struggled, because with this glimpse into the thinking of my child, I realized that he could not otherwise see himself in history because he plainly understood the horror of its association! What child would want to submit himself to slavery, or place himself back where his only option, considering his reality, was to be a slave? And yet, he dealt with rendering a solution for his history as he could only think of it. "What would life have been for him, for our family and for America, had slavery not happened?" he asked me after writing this. And I could not answer him, because I did not know how to take myself out of my history either. Of course, I also realized that like my son, I was a product of a somber hidden history, and agreed that there was no other place in time likewise that I feasibly could consider.

So, when he and I would read stories together, we decided not to get caught up in unrealistic fantasies about what it might have been like to be a medieval knight or a character in a Dickens novel. We agreed and accepted that we certainly could never have been Huck Finn, because we knew we were Jim, who was smarter anyway. Determinedly, we often searched for stories that presented a warrior personage of color such as Genghis Khan, or a tribal rebel like Nelson Mandela, because those legendary stories could provide us perhaps a bit of optimistic ethnic restitution. We, like other African American families were resigned to what we had no control of regarding our history, but, we believed the future could be different for our children. Were it not for the sanctification of slavery deeply woven into the American fabric, families like ours would not be agonizing still to establish counter narratives to restore respectability within the human tableau. This truth was so self-evident, my eleven-year-old could make sense of this concept without question. As did my seven-year-old son also, who inquiringly came upon us as we were studiously working to complete the application. My eldest had stated that the question asked of him was stupid. The younger, looked over his shoulder, read the question and agreed. "But I know what event I would have chosen!" he said slyly. "I would have gone back to the days of the Excalibur movie!" I looked at him puzzled. Excalibur was a favorite movie of his father's and mine. "Why, would you have been the Wizard Merlin?"

"No, Mom. I couldn't have been the Wizard. He was White! I would have been the Dragon instead, and eaten everybody all up!" He looked over at his brother, smiling with satisfaction. "Then, you wouldn't have to go back to Africa after all!" Caught up in the moment, my eldest replied, "Yeah, and then maybe I could be President one day, and not have to worry about getting shot at, isn't that right Mom?"

I made sure to deliver my son's application to the school the next morning. As limited as their knowledge of history was, I knew deep down in my soul that I needed to remain ever vigilant concerning the future of my sons. The residue of slavery was something they were beginning to parse and reluctantly understand as an inescapable element of their legacy, regardless that both of them were brought into the world with great ceremony. Given privileges as a physician, my husband assisted in their deliveries, being the first to smile at them before they were cleaned up and handed to me. As each was swaddled, my mother made sure to place a crisp brand new twenty-dollar bill in their tiny hands. Although sweetly poignant, she felt doing so was a good omen to foreshadow their future success, believing this gesture symbolized how far from the harsh circumstances and turmoil of births generationally our family had come. She also thought, in her Celtic way, that this signal would serve as a protective talisman. But given the outlook regarding unchanging, uncompromising, unyielding, social and professional referendums associated with constraining the capabilities of Black men nonetheless, omen or no, the protective value of my mother's twenty-dollar safeguard will surely need to become powerfully compounded miraculously, beyond any foreseen or imagined market call.

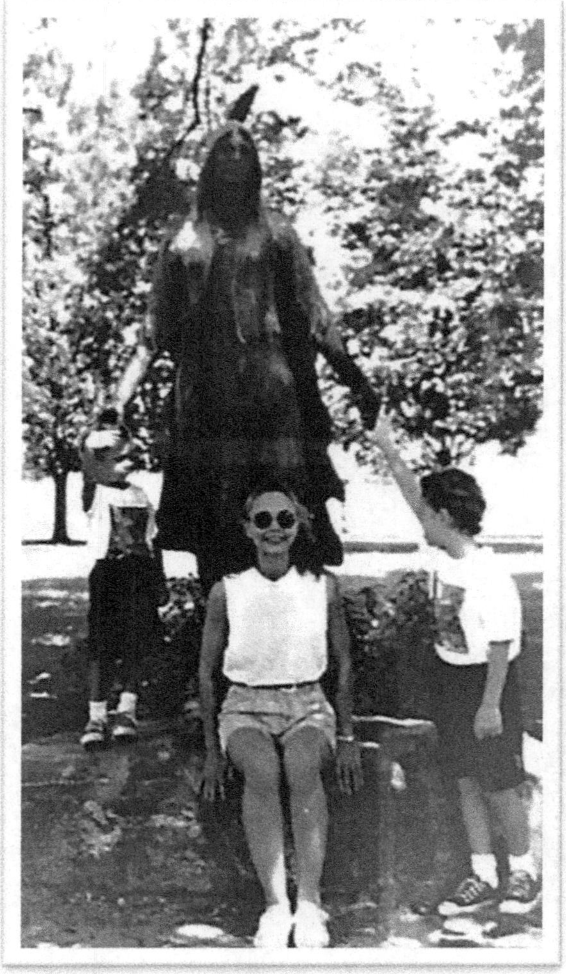

INTRODUCING MY SONS TO
THEIR POCAHONTAS ROOTS IN
JAMESTOWN, VA.

THE DINNER
LESSON 10: PATIENCE

Within the six thousand square feet that I called home, there were three remote wireless phones, but only one that could be found at any one time by the naked eye. The other two were magically invisible with force fields such that they were never located when I needed them. This meant that when my phone rang, like it did that afternoon, I ran from room to room and typically answered breathing heavily. Of course, my husband did not understand the reasoning behind the fact that this was the way it would be until I found the wherewithal and time to replace the entire system and start over. Until then, I contended that we all benefited from the exercise, and with caller ID we could easily determine if the run was worth it.

But of course, all my best girlfriends easily got through. This time it was Renee. "Hey Sweetie!"

Renee was my road dog. We had known each other for over twenty-five years and since she had just moved to Los Angeles, we tried to get together often. "Well, what are our plans for Monday night?" she asked. I thought quickly, knowing that my schedule in the evening was usually clear. I was one of those wives with a husband who typically worked late, so Monday night looked good. "I'm good for Monday, what's the plan?"

"How about we go to the Timberwolves game? I just got tickets, so you can be my date!" We joked often about being each other's best dates, because the way we figured it, we could both count on an evening well spent without any other agenda. That was what happened when you knew someone for twenty-five years. "Cool," I said. Looking at my brown couch and noticing that my orange cat had shed a good deal of cat hair which I would have to spend some of my afternoon cleaning off, I found that I wished Monday night was right then. "Okay, so you want me to drive? I can get us there in about fifteen minutes from my house." "Sounds good to me, girl. I'll be tired of driving anyway by six-thirty. The game starts at seven, so I'll be at your house by six. See ya!"

"Okay, kisses!" And I put down the phone only God knows where for the next time someone chose to call. Great. I had plans for Monday night, and the kids and my husband would just have to find a way to make it without me. Ha!

Many who met me, thought I did not work. They thought I sat at home doing I don't know what, but whatever it was, it surely included shopping, spas and chocolates. They were only half correct. Most people who truly knew me, knew that I worked my ass off! I built my own business, and could run most of the administrative operations from my house. That allowed me to flexibly schedule my time so that should I have wanted to shop, go to the spa or eat bon-bons during the day, well I sure as hell could. In addition, of course I managed the household--which ensured my husband and children ate well, and that my youngest son had the best chauffer service in town. I wish I had someone drive me everywhere in a new Mercedes! Well maybe in my old age I could look forward to that, but my son Quinn surely got the best end of the deal. And he had the nerve to lay the seat back as far as it would go, and plug in his ear buds so that he wouldn't have to listen to me during the drive. He wasn't slick though. I knew him. And I also knew that when he was in my car, he couldn't go anywhere but be with me for the next forty or so minutes. So, when I wanted to find out about his day or his life, the car held him captive. Of course, I could unplug those ear buds at any time, and I sometimes did.

I did have a great life! I also had the greatest girlfriends in the world. Honestly, I couldn't go through a day without their voices in my ear. We operated such that each provided balance in the life of the other, so that the world could be a happy place for those that loved us. Let me be the first to confirm that they guaranteed I rarely had an unpleasant day.

I couldn't wait to tell the boys and Rod, my husband, that I was going to the basketball game without them. Now, understand that in my household, "Sports" was not an airhead discussion when the conversation got to me. I was known throughout our circle of friends for an uncanny ability to choose the right Super Bowl team and NBA championship team every single year! "How did I do it?" they all wondered. It might have seemed beyond understanding, but during March Madness I was no joke. In fact, the truth was that I listened well throughout the season to what the fellows had to say, and then interjected the subtle things I observed about what they didn't say. Trust me that winning was more than just the right preparation and practice. Everything had to hit on all cylinders. The uniforms had to look right and the ratio of the team's hunger, versus humility, versus arrogance had to be on point. Then I factored in the other things, like team standings and whether I liked the players individually. Worked for me!

In fact, I was really excited to go out Monday night because I had been boycotting the Lakers and basketball games since Shaq left. For me, it was never a question of whether he or Kobe was the better "baller." What did matter was that the Laker games used to be so much fun. Being a fan was like being invited to one big party, with the last dance during the fourth quarter. You could yell and scream and boo and stand and clap and just be wild along with everyone else. When Shaq left, that atmosphere left too, and I lost interest. So, I went to see the other teams I liked when they come to town, or as in this case, I went to see the Other Team. Either way, I hadn't been to a game in a while, so I was looking forward to it.

I got another phone call from Renee later in the week. It went something like, "Sheli-baby, our plans have changed for Monday night."

"Oh no, Renee!" I sighed. Oh well, some other time, I thought to myself. "What happened?"

"Wait a minute, we are still going...we're just changing how we are rolling, that's all!" Renee laughed that impish little laugh she had, and now

I knew something was up. "Okay, just spill it," I said. I was always the impatient one.

"My dear friend," she began in her best English affectation, "You and I are to be the guests of Rob Silverman for dinner, and then the game. I just got a call—." Hold up, Renee could be a little crazy sometimes, so I had to test this conversation to determine where she was taking me...but even this sounded beyond her normal. "Renee," I said, "do you still want me to drive or do we now have a limo too?" "Oh, no honey," she replied dropping back to her southern flavored drawl, "I couldn't let it appear like I was expecting too much, so you'll still have to drive. And on top of that, I need to sell these other tickets I'm holding because I think we have better seats now. Do you know of anyone I could get to take the tickets?" Honestly, the thought of my husband and one of the guys did flash across my mind. But I came to my senses quickly. The whole point of Monday night, Rob Silverman or not, was that the evening out was tagged just for me. So I said, "No, Renee, I can't think of anybody. What time will you be at the house?"

"You know, I think five o'clock is better, that way we won't be late." This was true. "Okay. Kisses!"

All right, time for the next tier of phone calls. I had to figure out what to wear. Cydna wasn't home. Lisa Marie was in New York with her daughter who was on a modeling assignment. Geneviève was at work, so that left Brooke who was home, or at least kept her cell phone ringer on loud always for just these emergencies. She immediately understood. "You need to be impeccable, girl! But on the other hand, don't look available, you know? I hear he thinks he's a player!" Of course, I was married, as in long time married, so this advice made sense. Yet, our crew was not the dowdy married kind anyway. "Alright Brooksie, what comes to mind?"

"Well, I am thinking of a cute suit. You don't have to buy anything new, but if you did, I saw some really great sweater jackets at the boutique a couple of days ago. Let me know if I need to pick one up for you this weekend, if your closet isn't working out." See, this is why I loved my girls. All I had to do was ask, and my fashion needs were met. “Oh, don’t wear any heels you can’t be in for a long time, but some little boots would be cute too.” There, my stylist had spoken. No doubt, I would be coming correct! Now, with that matter done, I could call the rest of my sisters later, and just gloat. But it would be a shared gloat, where the heart glows from the connection. It was Thursday, so I had to be sure to wash and blow-dry my hair by Saturday. That way, it would look about right, with no fly-a-ways. I have “in-between” hair. This means that I must deal with it so that I can plan for the time when it will look its best. Alright, the plan was down. The weekend could roll in with no problems.

And it did. Monday was a day filled with my normal run arounds with business errands and Quinn errands. Of course, I knew I had to put up with Quinn’s vocal disappointment about having to eat fast food instead of a real dinner, but he would live. My oldest, Rhys, was nonchalant as always about the fact that I even had a plan of my own. He would find something in the refrigerator to eat before his classes. Rod, on the other hand could eat at the clinic before he came home, so he was good to go. Renee was on time at five, parked her car in my driveway, jumped into mine and we whooshed smoothly down Olympic Boulevard to the Figueroa parking lot like clockwork. Our tickets were waiting at the Will Call.

We had plenty of time and thought the Will Call booth wait would take just a few minutes. But it of course was our luck to be behind the wrong people. You know the kind, the ones with issues about not being able to pick up tickets "which should have been left for them." The two women in front of us were at the booth window so long, they could have also made hotel reservations! Actually, I was suspect about where they were trying to go anyway, because they could not possibly be dressed for a game. One of them had on short-shorts and a bomber jacket, with cowboy boots. But they were expensive boots, so I supposed she had somewhere to go after all. We finally got our tickets and quickly went to the VIP door. The escalator to the restaurant was easy to find, and the hostess knew our table was waiting.

It looked like a table for a medieval king. It was long, seated for about twenty-five guests on each side. We were escorted to the head of the table and were seated across from each other with Mr. Silverman's chair between us. I'm telling you it was as close to a royal seating as we would ever get in our little lifetimes. And when the King entered the room, you would have thought that all the humble serfs knew that the best time to be near him was tonight, because they were all there jockeying for manly handshakes and good seats. It was an incredible sight! Renee and I got to witness it all up close and personally. Mr. Silverman graciously introduced everyone to us, and wouldn't you know it, remarkably, his eyes were on Renee the whole time. In fact, everyone else may have been in that room, but he had come to dine with Renee. At least that is how it looked, and I kicked her under the table because she was now sitting very straight in her chair, looking like she was oblivious to that one huge vibe of the evening. I wanted her to know that I had not missed it, and that I had her covered. Instantly, I knew then this was why she invited me along in the first place. She of course looked beautiful. And Mr. Silverman at nearly eighty, seemed confident that he was still in his prime. Fine. I excused myself to get Renee and myself our dinner plates from the buffet. I approached the table politely with, "Shall we see what's at the Salad Bar, Renee?" for a needed but plausible momentary escape. Renee is one of those girlfriends that not only had a sense of humor, but also could readily apply it to most things in life. Dinner that night was certainly to be one of those things. If you have ever been a Black person who wondered what White people, those of the enormously powerful persuasion, thought of us as race in total, then this evening would have been your jackpot. I would offer that our experience may not have been exclusive to humanity, but I was glad that we would get ours served in small enough doses so that we could keep progressing through the evening. I for one, wanted to see how this would end. We would be introduced to and dine with the owner of the city newspaper, the developer of major projects on the Westside of town, the head of the largest homeless shelter, and a host of other men of position and influence. We would not necessarily know what the significance the game was to them, other than the chance to get out like we were doing for an enjoyable time together. They certainly knew each other well and enjoyed each other's company immensely. Renee and I had been invited into their circle for the evening and had been given ringside seats.

As one introduction would be made, conversation would begin with another, to the point that there probably were about ten conversations circling above heads waiting a turn to be pulled down to the table for their moment. Everyone loved the minority charity that Renee represented. So much so, that they all offered to be involved and help in any big way. "So, what would you like me to do Renee? Host a dinner here at the club for $500 to $1000 bucks a ticket, for what, say about twenty-five people right here at this table? What do you think about that for starters?"

I could hear Renee's brain turning. Yes, that might do for starters, but the proposal she had in mind was a longer termed partnership, and I knew she wanted to find the way to work that scenario in. But before she could, another introduction occurred. This person might also provide major assistance, "...Because the problem in the African American community is so enormous!" That was when it happened. One of them turned to Renee for her explanation. Honestly, I saw her big brown eyes blink rapidly in disbelief, but then again, who would see this coming? I couldn't catch that ball for her! No, it was too fast for me too. I continued eating my delicious Thai beef entrée. "Hit it back over the net, Renee," was the thought I willed her. The owner of the conversation at this juncture was the Twilight Mission man. He rattled off the figures he lived with day to day: that while

African Americans constituted merely only 11% of the population, they starkly comprised over 50% of the homeless population in the city. He discussed his concern about the correlated problem of the drug addiction to cocaine that often was coupled with the homeless issue, given that his Center was targeted to recovery and rehabilitation. I could attest to the fact that he was truly concerned and seemed to be a caring person. I felt for him. He was trying to gain funding for one of his priority projects from Mr. Silverman also, and was seemingly close to achieving his goal based upon their long-term relationship.

I didn't want to generalize, but I couldn't help it. Truly, things were done in a much different way when there were moneyed people involved. I was not ashamed to say it, but I was drinking it all in. I kept my ear tuned to Renee the entire time, because I was her date and protector. I was trying to figure out which potential relationships could have been of benefit to her that evening.

I put my fork down. I had to. Because another voice loudly exclaimed, "...And what is wrong with your Black Men? Why can't they just take care of their children and homes?" Looking up from my plate and putting down my fork, I saw that it was Mr. Silverman who had just finished confidently and concretely mouthing these words. Having directed those of his court to other ends of the table, he had finally taken his seat between Renee and me for dinner. He stated to us that he really didn't understand this situation because the societal impacts were just so clearly obvious. I looked right at him, searching for the soul behind the eyes and found that he truly meant every world. His were not racist remarks (right!). These were statements of his impartial beliefs and personal observations, he intimated. Yet those statements took me to a place in my brain where I wondered what it must be like to be him. I wondered what life must be like, to live so compassionately (his perspective), but untouched by this problem. I wished I could have been the Lord Jesus Christ himself in this strange turn of conversation, because I wanted to answer the man with something that could provoke the discussion of a caring human solution. It seemed to me, that people with this much money could entertain the scope of a resolution beyond anything I could ever dream of or expect to impact. But to him, I was just a woman, an unimportant Black woman, and window dressing at that.

Some would say that my style of heartfelt and direct conversation was more aggressive than most unimportant Black women. The reason for this was simple. My father raised me. I certainly brought up the point that not all Black men abandoned their children. "Goodness! Those I knew of were extremely responsible..." "...Well, we don't want to discuss the rare cases such as yours," washed over me in reply. The food had been not necessarily great, but dinner was now getting interesting. I wanted to scream aloud, "Bring it on!" Instead, I took a drink short of a gulp to keep quiet. I could almost hear the liquid speaking to me, "Down girl! Don't scare him!" So instead of engaging in verbal tennis with this man, I let him continue on as I ate the food he was paying for. "…You know, I am convinced that the key is education! Your people need to see that education is their way out, and I want to do everything I can do to support you." He was trying to do his best to explain himself. Renee and I politely, blandly accommodated his explanations throughout the remainder of dinner, interrupted only by the game's start. On top of that, to add insult to injury, the Other Team lost.

Shell-shocked, Renee whispered, "Girl, you know we need to make sense of this night, right?" Renee and I were tired and a bit overwhelmed from the evening, but at the same time we were wired still from our shared disbelief. Incredibly, we knew that we would never be the same again. Not that we were ever cavalier about our lives, but to know that we had been close enough to have seen the face of a lion in the jungle and not flinch, well, that is life changing. What we found out was that the lion was not going to eat us, because we were no threat to him. He lived his life despite the nuisances we caused around him. He thought he was wiser and fiercer than we. He thought he had nothing to fear. And no, we did not flinch, because we perceived correctly that he was too bored with our kind to give chase anyway.

"Can you believe he wanted to put an article in the paper with my picture on it, so that I would put our men on blast? Can you believe it!" Renee was flabbergasted, still in amazement at the evening's end. "Yes, I know it's hard to imagine, but we really were there, and that really did happen," I agreed with her, sleepily. We were standing outside on the driveway at my house, not ready to say goodbye yet. "But I will say one thing, he liked you a lot, girl. I knew he was sick of me. I was just supposed to be your shadow. Not!"

"That's okay. I planned that," and there came the mischievous Renee laugh, even though she tried to yawn. "Can you just picture tonight if I had gone alone? Did you not see that we were the only women at that table? No girl, I knew you would have my back. They are all like that, as you well know. They all think they want a taste of brown sugar, but not tonight, and not from me—No, I don't get my business done like that!" It was late, and she had to go to a breakfast meeting early the next morning. Mutually, we agreed to call it a night.

I opened the front door to a dark, sleeping quiet of my household, but turned back to see that the moon shone brightly upon Renee's car under my lone redwood tree. We hugged goodnight. Of course, we would talk about this in the morning. She had about a thirty-minute drive home from my house, and I knew she would climb into bed as soon as she got there. Once inside, I shut the lights off downstairs, and carefully crept up the steps so as not to awaken my children, but then again, burglars would not awaken my children at that hour. Retiring, I rubbed lavender lotion on my hands, which always drifted me to sleep, and tried to softly slip under my blankets.

"How'd your evening go?" my husband asked the empty night air above my head. I didn't know he had been awake, waiting up for me. "Oh, it went great," I sighed dreamingly. "Mr. Silverman said you were a rarity."

"What? What the hell does that mean?" the voice on the pillow next to me asked in a highly charged reply. "I don't really know, dear." My eyes were closing. I spoke without seeing or wanting to have a lengthy conversation. I was at the point of trying to command sleep into my brain, almost there. "Honestly, I don't even think Mr. Silverman knows what he meant when he said it. He wasn't trying to be offensive dear, it just came up in the discussion, that's all."

"You were talking about me? How'd I come up?" My magnificent husband's voice was awake and exasperated, but on the other hand, I think he was gladly surprised that he had been a focus of conversation. He liked to hear about himself, like most men did. "You didn't really. He was talking about how Black men shirk their responsibilities for their children and families, and how they were so irresponsible…"

"…And you let him get away with that shit?" My husband was now fully alert, sitting up, no longer speaking to the darkness but nudging me so that I would not find sleep after all. "No dear, of course I didn't, come on now," I assured. "But regardless of what I said, I don't think I changed his mind. He really doesn't get it. He lives in a fantasy world where he doesn't have to…"

"Fuck him! That's just how most White boys think! Why would you expect him to be any different?" And that was the absolute end of that conversation.

Well, now that my husband was up, he grabbed for the remote on the nightstand and turned on the TV. Unfailingly, there was always a manly war movie on at one in the morning. I had become an expert in self-hypnosis whenever action movies blasted across the screen at ungodly hours of the late night, so I easily found quick, deep sleep with bombs exploding over continents.

A CONVENING
LESSON 11: COMPASSION

I gasped aloud in the middle of prayer! I would have never believed it, had I not seen it for myself, and had I not engaged my "partner in crime." My co-conspirator was considered by many to be the most distinguished and esteemed theologian and peacemaker in the city of Los Angeles. With a deeply melodic, measured resonance, he artfully and benevolently implored everyone at their tables to stand, and to take hold of the hand of the person next to them, and to join in a Prayer of Affirmation. In clearly articulated unison, four hundred and fifty handsomely dressed attendees professed a necessity for the cultural vitality of their beloved university's Black alumni, assuring validation of their shared institutional legacy and support for an inclusive future. Directed hand holders included the president, his senior cabinet, faculty, staff, students and vested highly involved members of the Black alumni community...

Weeks earlier, I gleefully asked my revered eighty-something activist friend when I proposed the battle plan, "Can you just picture it?" After the dinner event was over, he said that I was "called of God" but that was only because he loves me. Others would not say that yet would certainly say instead that I had nerve beyond comprehension, since when he called everyone to action, he stated that this challenge indeed was my noble request of him, and of them. It is now way too late to admonish me for insisting everyone go outside of their comfort zones, but I firmly believe that there is no growth until emotional stretching can occur. Yes, I waited for fallout, but I feel that in these precariously crude times, any notion regarding "Diversity" should be unpacked to include the raw cultural insight that motivates and shapes it. To ignore this lens, or to mitigate it within broader "diversity constructs," disrespects meaningful touchstones. Yet, it is this lens that is most always ignored--

which is why I needed to rely upon prayer to make the point as a first step.

I acquiesced to a request from my vice president to host a dinner event for the fortieth anniversary celebration of the organization I have had the privilege to lead for some years. Atypical of most ethnic alumni organizations, I stopped doing "dinners" because of several factors which included exorbitant costs, little return and limited outreach returns across the shrinking national demographic of Black alumni minted by the university. The cohort behavior pattern indicated that it was largely disengaged with the university because enrollment and graduation rates of Black students continued to unacceptably decline, and were now at a level of not being able to sustain a critical mass. Consequently, while the past models of our fundraising had been to honor celebrated alumni, the pool of our noteworthy alumni was quietly shrinking and had been wearing thin. Most Black alumni with significant achievement had already been celebrated by the organization in prior years, and the remaining pool of subsequent generationally distinctive alumni was rising at a much slower rate. Importantly too, the climate regarding Black student inclusion on campus was growing emotively hotter and hotter by the year. Thus, I could not be credibly authentic about a celebratory, positional dinner event especially when the winds of needed institutional change were blowing. In its place for several years, my organization instead hosted campus-wide ethnic cultural arts productions that were magnificently appreciated and attended, being received as educationally noteworthy by a broad swath of campus groups. Our track record of providing high-quality events with hosted receptions was considered innovative, to the satisfaction of our sponsors and donors who were tired of dinners anyway.

However, with the fortieth-year celebration, I believed I could position the organization within the current dynamic of campus controversy as a useful and required resource. In my own academic research on Black alumni agency, leadership and engagement, a survey of our board leaders clearly suggested that most Black alumni were deeply concerned about the lack of Black diversity and equity in faculty, administrative leadership, and peer-to-peer student campus and classroom experiences. Consequently, their generationally prolonged predispositions were highly associated with a resulting collective lack of institutional trust and engagement. The survey also suggested that with this being the case, alumni wished to be included as important partners in new diversity policy planning strategies, given their own life experiences and relationships with students as mentors, sponsors, parents and donors. Although the senior administration of the university was not open to this kind of input regarding diverse alumni, I was sometimes asked to provide my administrative perspective in limited open faculty meetings. I pursued this narrow path of forward motion with my voice used as one communally representative of our board. It was in this vein that we finally agreed to do a dinner event, with the condition being that it would set the tone for our future involvement by demonstrating our distinctive reach, influence and seriousness concerning the goal of improving institutional social justice.

To understand the underlying ebb and flow of the Black alumni heartbeat at most elite, highly selective, predominately White institutions today is to hear a humming-- and then a roar of outrage regarding the cycles of institutional racism and classroom discrimination that are still unbroken. To also be the parents of bright, hopeful Black children within these traditionally conservative environments is to fear for their socialization and their development into young adulthood. To assuage such fears, it becomes critical to find that campus resource which can be trusted and relied upon as some sort of cultural anchor. It is surely the case that our young are still one of few in the classrooms, and often left out of study groups and student networks of entitlement and privilege. To enable successful outcomes in the face of these kinds of inequities, this resource must deeply affirm value and self-esteem, as well as model resilience, persistence, grit and success. Our Black alumni organization is one such primary resource for students of color in my university.

...I requested my Reverend to command that everyone hold hands during the invocation. I wanted to compel an experience of compassion one could touch, and I knew the he was the man for the job. The grand ballroom decor was resplendently beautiful, decorated in gold and bronze brocades, with accents of white orchids and green English ivy. The ceilings were gilded in a gleaming silver patina, with crystal-beaded chandeliers. Reception guests could wistfully sip beverages on the breezy deck of the marina, with an early spring sunset dropping into the Pacific. The awards stage was a shock of bronze lame, haute floral and up lighting. Stunning, perfect, breathtakingly overloaded sensory backdrops to emphasize Black amazingness.

All eyes were closed in prayer, but I peeked. To see a room of four hundred and fifty university people clasping hands, united in a moment of mutual respect, was a personal moment of jubilation. Where my stalwartly skeptical Black alumni constituents had been loath to trust the sympathies of the institution, and rightly so, at this moment they too could sense the presence of an optimistic possibility in the room. Where the senior level cabinet administrators were the outsiders with few relationships in this room, they had to forthrightly acknowledge a mutual spark of faith now being bestowed upon them to suitably do those right things to stimulate progressive change. The salad was fantastically blessed with Hope.

The evening unfolded our narrative as a gift to all in attendance. Each important and celebrated honoree wove precious threads of resilience throughout their remarks, creating a blazing patchwork reminder that while the experiential input considered from culturally underrepresented stakeholders does not yet exist at the strategic policy level in predominately

White institutions, it should. Currently, diversity policy implementation at predominately White institutions is evaluated, judged and measured with admissions rates and enrollment yields by using cursory gross percentage levels, allowing university leadership to often argue that metrics overall have been achieved. But this ideal does not serve the best interests of underserved Black constituencies in this millennium, or their future. Rather, diversity policy that empathizes with the ambitions of Black success, and aligns solutions informed by disaggregated racial data and trends reviewed for positive benefit, would be truly transformational.

Marvelously, the evening's notable honorees confirmed how racial and cultural stakeholders should have their stories heeded, and the lessons within them obliged. In prodigious effect, their journeys were not translated or watered down for validation, as if to describe water to us other fish in the room. Instead, a value proposition for Black alumni to believe that inclusion at their alma mater could be more than symbolic was struck and offered. That a brilliant disruption of policy modeling had been presented for later reflection that night was an underestimation of intention, much like the after effects of a good wine. Adeptly maneuvered but without duplicity, Affirmation was served as a refreshing mid-course sorbet, clearing the palate for a savory evening of breaking bread together, breaking stereotypes and breaking through.

ZEBERT!© VICTORIOUS
LESSON 12: FORTITUDE

I relish my exquisite touchstones of each season, but especially the summers when I hear the mountains calling to me, offering sanctuary. In Virginia, there is an Appalachian trail I walk like a pilgrimage upon each visit. Along its path, I experience an unfolding security in the rolling hills quite otherwise than my father did, since the air I exultantly breathe no longer reeks with past deaths for sport or longing. I stretch my arms out in communion with the trees and grasp for wide spans of liberty differently than my grandparents ever dreamed, yet I dare not compare my amusements with the sober necessities of how careful they were to move quietly through living. It is truly fascinating to comprehend that I can look at the same grand hillsides with a sight which perceptively cuts through time, legacy and claim.

Always gathering meditative assuagement from this bewitching landscape that we would leave behind, my brother and I long ago each packed a carefully chosen trail rock in our suitcases, to sneak back home the smells of green walks along this trail, celebrations of lazy summer picnics at Hungry Mother park, familiar hugs from all the grandparents and cousins, and smoky jars filled with prized lightning bugs. One quick way to put a smile on my face is to look at that rock. I keep a rock collection in an antique gilded display case in my house, no kidding. It honors many beloved memories of my adventured life, and metaphorically reminds me that despite innumerable obstructions my family encountered in the face of historical attempts to normalize recriminations for being Black—wholly or fractionally--I can hold in my hand and connect firmly with something that defied constraints of time and human infirmity regardless.

Because racism in this country has been such a proxy for abhorrence across the breadth of my bloodline, I cannot easily or unconditionally ignore, or casually forgive, the tremendous injury caused in the wake of my family's calls and responses to love. To bring forth any such inferred interpretation causes a pernicious anger within me that cannot be calmed by an expected or presumed political correctness. I am confronted with palpable memories daily, if not several times throughout a day, of my mother's emotional fragility and my father's decided isolation from the mainstream. I must respect that these states became the patent remnants of their individual preservation and coping mechanisms just to remain functional citizens. Will that be me too? I wonder if one day I will also require some kind of psychological salve, perhaps a mystic elixir, drunk to numb ever worsening realizations that the elimination of racism in America will require an act of God.

Similarly, as my parents did, I felt targeted and compromised often in my youth by the isolating stigmas of society. Hence, I created a phantom reality in which racial puzzles could be deliberated intelligently and thoughtfully. In my teenage years, my alter ego was named "Zebert! ©," a little green zebra that could not be easily seen but could appear to others when he wanted just by stepping out of tall grasses. Zebert!© was green because in the grass, he was easily mistaken for shadows. His green striped fur blended with the grass, and alternately his black fur gave the shadows depth. Zebert!© absolutely captured my spirit because he might be standing right in front of you, yet not be seen precisely. Needless to say, I felt that way, not just because I was young, but because my racial dispensation was so historically maligned, rather than seen for the victory it was. The name Zebert!© was chosen with great intention, as the definition of a "zebert" is to be the smartest person in the room. I always enjoyed the play on words, knowing that most people would never discern the real meaning of the name, and would simplistically limit their thinking to the obvious and superficial association to the physicality of the animal. He was no ordinary character for many reasons, but primarily because he imbued a distinctive vital independence and individuality. Yet unlike my zebra, I had no place to hide. My children, now grown, also embraced Zebert! © as their own special character from the stories I wrote for them, stuffed animals I created and clothes I designed for them to wear with Zebert! © logos. Zebert! © brightly shines in my psyche from time to time, but like the rocks I collected he is merely a symbol, and cannot mend dilemmas caused by racial phobias because he is not real.

Since the tensions and hierarchies of race and culture astonishingly continue to justify mass degradation and ruin, the world certainly could use Zebert! © today! In his place, a new industry of "Diversity" has bubbled to the surface as the current tool of choice to categorize and resolve mounting social climate issues. For my part, instead of summoning Zebert! ©, I have been left to personally contemplate a differing degree of restitution. Try as I might to apply the quandary, for those of my ken, the conversations everyone else is having just do not apply. There is quite a difference between speaking about the beatitudes of newly proposed intra-racial and cultural relationships, versus living interracially and consequentially. Only those that have been bestowed this life, as well as pioneered through it, know what the truths of successful resolution really are, and how they should be distilled and applied. Most often when asked for insight on race and place, I am not given the platform to speak as being multiracial, nor am I heard as if a multiracial perspective can be associatively valuable.

It astounds me to consider the rarity of my parents' marriage because I find nothing out of order with their desires to be striving individuals, and loving parents. Yet not being blind to the historical paucity of the circumstance, at this stage of my life I am now coming to terms with realities that cannot be negotiated, as an era is about to pass. Fatalistically, I am preparing for a state of consciousness that when my parents are both physically gone, their guarantees for my comfort will be absent, and will leave me anchorless in a muddled world. No matter the distances between us caused by their mindfulness about where I could live a safe and uncontested life, for nearly twenty-one thousand days we have seen the same sun at daybreak and come nightfall, said goodnight to same moon. I have been loved beyond all galaxies, and now I presciently await the flickering silences of their constellations. What I mean to say is that with their daily waking, my smash and bang throughout life without apology is protected, and manifests within a continuum dependably overseen by them for me. I have lived an Affirmed life out loud because of their revolutionary points of view, which particularly treasured racial and cultural distinction. I have been confidently courageous because I have witnessed a different truth than most. because they boldly visioned one to life. Their stalwart, unconditional and purpose-filled encouragement invigorated me to believe I was deserving of everything I aspired to and somehow accomplished, without any required explanation of my humanity.

From my birth, I have been inculcated in the belief that there is no justice without the kind of peace only assured through racial connection and transference. My firsthand experiences are only a part of the measure of what is possible, or what should come with time. I exist at the beginning of a building trend that has not peaked yet, and may not be accepted for some years, although it is generationally climbing at a rate faster than ever identified or acknowledged before. As a possible proof, the universe is becoming more multiracial and multicultural every second of every day. This is an evolution that is happening with quiet surprise, and the world census is beginning to reflect this shift with a statistical meaning. Yet, given these trends, coupled with international research of my own, the world's grand challenge to foundationally align color and culture still seems exasperatingly beyond the grasp of the most intelligent minds. I believe this is because the circumstance of an affirmed racial neutrality has rarely been observed, assessed, or truthfully and safely discussed. But for those of us who have certainly lived to tell it, the outcome with most significance is to prove that racial peace is without a doubt within the natural order of things.

I have always used educational opportunities to further my subjective experiences regarding ethnic and cultural intersectionality, unafraid to be my own test case. I obtained my doctorate in Global Education Policy and in doing so, had the privilege to do research in Hong Kong and Abu Dhabi. By the time I entered my studies, I had already been around the world several times, always curious concerning the basis for global perceptions about the American descendants of slaves, which were usually substantively negative and misinformed. I wondered too, about how ideals of inclusion were defined and normalized within other emerging ethnic societies. In my travels, I would directly question and discuss these concepts informally with people I would meet, having the most intriguing conversations, largely also because meeting "someone like me" was a first for them. Within formal study, I confirmed that throughout global societies, the multiracial, multicultural group perspective was always a suppressed, offensive objective, and never considered as a needed or determining factor for policymaking which purported to address societal improvement. Unfortunately, it seems this early millennium continues to miss opportunities to create needed frameworks to unsettle pedantic conversations about race and culture, to release many of these dialogues from myth and shame, and accurately reflect history. In the case of the United States, it has only been fifty years that interracial marriages have been legal, and only seventeen since the census allowed a multiracial classification. But no platform has emerged that knows what to do with this data, how to use it for social benefit, or why it would be important to evaluate. History has wrecked itself with racial carnage in effort to infuse mainstream progress. But today's actualities should no longer be minimized and used instead as points for great learning that fosters world view change.

My prayer for what remains of my life is simply an earnest one: that I will witness with my loved ones a final baton pass and carry in this treacherous ideology contest for privilege and overcoming. I speculate that winning will be a quiet occasion, due to uncountable, catastrophic false starts and losses. I would like to believe that a symbolic Finish Line could be effusively marked with Evident Truths and staked blazingly with Affirmation. My hope is that crossing it will feel as satisfying and victorious as we -- my parents, my family, Zebert! © and I -- imagined it.

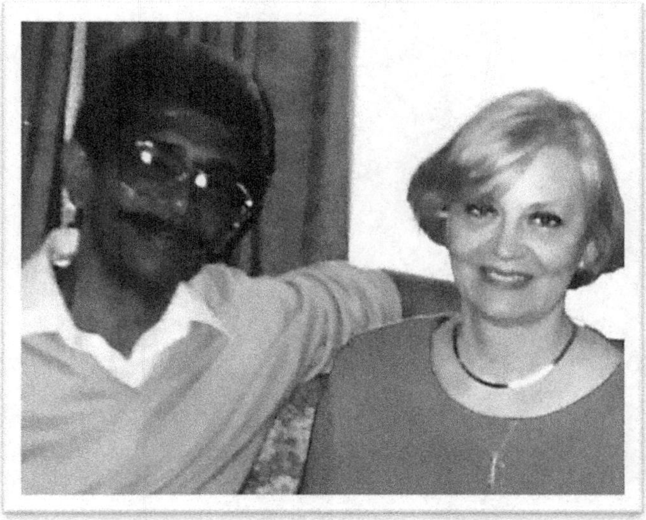

DAD AND MOM BACK "HOME" IN VIRGINIA.
AN UNBREAKABLE, ENDURING FRIENDSHIP.

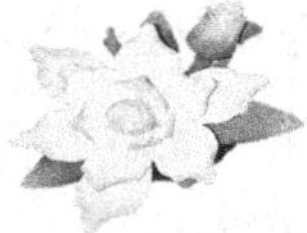

WILDFLOWER
LESSON 13: FORGIVENESS

I knew when I spied it, the lone grey boulder jutting singularly from the water's edge would be my quiet place to celebrate, so I precariously trekked over the clinging seaweed and gluts of whirlpools to reach my destination before the tides fully swept in. I could have sworn it hailed me from afar, rather, it was just my own curiosity beckoning, then taunting me, about whether I would overcome my usual paralyzing timidity at being seen in solitude, especially while other tourists happily meandered randomly by in groups briskly taking in the shore before sunset. But I had come here on a mission, to lay my burdens down and give thanks. My petite bottle of champagne was in my backpack, along with the small Waterford flute I had so carefully packed. I had to hurry now, the sun would set soon, so I ventured faster over the rocks and hastened my climb.

Kicking away and flattening loose gravel, I sat down Indian-style, absolutely in awe of the violent transforming of the ocean greens and blues reflecting from the sky and then tumbling into foam upon the sand. The crashing waves obscured any other sounds I could possibly focus upon, serving as the perfect reminder that I had come to this place with momentous purpose. I unpacked my dusty pack and lay upon the ground a towel I had taken from the hotel room, my glass, and bottle that I opened with little circumstance. We were going to toast, God and I. “Salud!” I said loudly to the glistening sparkles of the falling sunset. And I sat there for a while, oblivious to the nonchalant pitch and steps of the evening joggers down below, unthinkingly communing with twilight, gradually detecting the simmering heat of the boulder seeping through my cargo pants, the light powder of swept gravel upon my feet and hands, and the sprays of surf that splashed upwards catching through the ringlets of my hair. I slowly breathed in what I hoped were elements that could cleanse away and revitalize whatever remained of an exhausted brain. I had driven fifty miles, remembering the august beauty of this place from prior visits with friends, taking note it should be exactly where I could come to reverently acknowledge the bargain I had made long ago. As I watched the ocean waves form instantaneously one upon the other, I was soothed into exquisite recollections of being just as free as they to rise and collide and land upon a moment that could effortlessly be either creation or destruction. My life's care and patience were crystallized in such moments, now evidenced by a seemingly indomitable resilience over the years.

My outlook on life was best stewarded through an acquired worship of nature, gifted to me in my youth. If we weren't languidly summering at my grandparents' homes or visiting with my mother, then my brother and I were rambling across the country, carefree hobo-style with my father. His preparation was meticulously quick and efficient, and we became well versed and apprenticed in the routine. Pop would take out the front seat of our Volkswagen Bug, and pack an ice cooler, cook stove, lantern, flashlight, cast iron pan, fishing poles and three sleeping bags in its space, and with the AAA map highlighting our journey in yellow, we were off! En route to a destination, he would drive until tired, and where we would stop would be where we would sleep. Sometimes it might be streamside, or a cow pasture, or at the bottom of a long dead volcano, tentless, under a blanket of stars. Our days were spent catching fish sitting still atop flat rocks on river banks, up to our knees casting lines, swimming and diving in those frigid rivers and lakes, hunting for frogs and crayfish, exploring mysterious caves and hiking dirt worn trails, reading favorite comic books while sunning ourselves into enviable copper tans, basking in the magnificence of nature and the wild. Our daring escapes served as buffers from the city living and social rules we were confined by. We believed we were untouchable, surrounded by majesty far from the recriminations of stultifying common jurisdiction, stodgy interpretation and plodding conformity. We were empowered with the purest vibrancies of undiluted independence. These primal, ancient resonances would fortify the agencies by which my brother and I could move successfully through the world, and were essential to our efficacious development and growth into the unshrinking people we later would become.

Back at home, with the unbound fortresses of mountain ranges and valleys far behind us, we faced a number of shocking affronts caused in the aftermath of social revolutions. There was the nondescript day otherwise when my brother and I walked home from school, urgently following the rising black smoke clouds over our neighborhood. Two fire trucks blocked our street, spewing water on the source. The clearing ash revealed that it was our car that had been torched by a roman candle not accidently, and we stood there watching it burn down to the frame because the fire engines couldn't salvage even the idea of it. Scared, yes. We knew someone was sending our father a message. Or, there was the unpreventable inevitability that our home would be burglarized each year, like clockwork, where when we turned our key in the lock, the living room drapes would billow wildly over the smashed window glass strewn violently on the carpet. We knew not to go inside, but to go next door and call the police, and wait on them to walk through our house in the darkness. Afterwards, our father would solemnly take inventory of what we had been left with sans televisions or sneakers, and we would sleep together in one bedroom that night. Because these kinds of frightening occurrences due to our father's activism could be expected and were non-fiction throughout our childhood and adolescence, we toughened up. I did not have to read the news about other people's trials and testimonies in the Movement. I had grown up being an eyewitness to anarchy and terrorism due to apartheid in the

United States, and I was a survivor. More importantly, I was unafraid to be a survivor, and accordingly learned to face my life head-on instead of becoming a deer in headlights. I learned that to be afraid was to lose the ability to think clearly in disaster. So, I took my brother's hand often in these situations and found a place for us to be calm and quiet. When we would leave the city behind on weekends or summers, I looked forward to floating on my blow-up raft on the Russian River with a slow current to nowhere.

I may have been hardened by events in an uncompromising life, but I did not reach adulthood unsentimental and without hope. I received many blessings with the journey, which was the reason I was here this day. Appreciatively, I sat quietly on my boulder and watched the prism of sundown brilliantly light, then fade into reds and purples, then dissolve and begin to sink. With the warmth of the dusk, I sipped my last champagne drops from my beautiful Waterford flute, a piece from my wedding crystal. I had long accepted I had been born into imperious debate regarding the visibly broken history of this country, and its implausibility concerning social and racial experimentation. Yet truth be told, I did tire from an imposed wear and tear of exercises to wrap my brain around schisms of my biracialness, but not because I was confused by any crisis of identity. I never struggled with inner conflicting demons of my Whiteness versus Blackness. I was overly assured by my parents' belief that I was perfectly and beautifully made, and this was superbly my reality. I never wished to be different, only that the world around me could be.

I was fortunate to be nurtured with abundant love and acceptance, yet the happiness of my parents was my constant worry. Clashes between their White versus Black worlds were relentless, but were not their fault. I was perpetually anxious that I could not safeguard them from cruelties that I did not understand, but could certainly feel and see the destruction from. This burden was too heavy for childhood, but I carried it under my skin nonetheless, and I never relaxed. From an early age, it was clear to me that few viewed my parents' marriage as a triumph of the human spirit, and I would watch them intensely as they contrived to win even simple conveniences. In all things, their motivations were "judged" and they had to "prove" they were worthy of decent courtesies: being eagerly assisted to buy a car, or generously shown a home in a picturesque neighborhood, or quickly seated well at a highly-starred restaurant to enjoy a night out together, or kindly aided to register us in school for gifted classes, or even cordially assisted when picking up portraits taken of me because I did not look like the child who could belong to either of them... I was a helpless bystander to the disintegration of my parents' utopian ideals for a better social order, and to the fractures of any deserved happiness of our family unit. To counter this, a determined and constant immersion with nature was my father's way to demonstrate to my brother and me that regardless, we could not hate God. How profound a realization it was to us that although we were left to survive at the mercy of lesser people, this same God created the splendor of the trees and mountains which gave us refuge and peace. Hence, my bargain was made so that animosity would not shatter me. I had to trust that my future held an extraordinary promise in return for an enduring and unsolvable anguish. You see, while my parents wished to live as if color did not matter, I plainly knew from the startling responses of others that it did.

My fate was released like a prayer, just weeks before my graduation from college when I encountered the miracle of my friend, later to be my husband. It may have taken the entire four years for me to really look at him differently, as a young man of goodness and substance, but there was that instant in our familiar camaraderie when I did exactly that. I appreciated his brilliance and values as being similar to those I had been raised with. His people were from the same area of country as my people, so he intuitively and viscerally understood the irony of my existence, although we met three thousand miles away from there. I sensed that he would not attempt to change me, and would respectfully honor me as an ambitious, intellectual, equal. Our dreams and aspirations were complementary, with his studies and passion for serving others as a physician, and mine as an entrepreneur and businessperson. With great humor and intention, we were to build a powerful alliance of love cemented by best friendship. Our lives have become indivisible and it is unfathomable one of us without the other, in true "ride or die" fashion, through our many episodes. We have grown up, and older, together.

Differently than I experienced, our sons have an ease of living, filled with laughter from a plentiful access to grandparents, aunts, uncles and cousins, whom all lovingly endorse and appreciate them. My husband and I made certain that their bedrock of life was buttressed and impenitent about the true phenomenal heritage, spectrum and sentiments of Black. We knew without any question that challenges to their entitlement and privileges would not be due to lack of exposure or inherited accomplishment, as both of us had grown up as middle-class children of Black professionals (his father being a commercial airline pilot, and mine a nuclear design engineer…), but could instead occur from a possibility of cowering to systemic negative ratifications of self. We were so fortunate to discover an all-Black elementary school where they attended from preschool until seventh grade. Our premise was that with the multitude of caring exemplars of racial excellence in their formative years, coupled with a formalized educational curriculum that clearly articulated and entwined intersections of their ethnicity and culture, our sons' human identities would be ineradicably forged and affirmed. As duly planned, they have grown into confident men, well poised for their greatness. And I have begun to breathe.

Cool winds folded around me like a blanket, and with the slip of the sun into obscurity, I carefully made my way back to the hotel suite for the evening. While 'my memories were bottomless still waters, this journey had not been foolhardy. I had come to celebrate the meaning of my mother's life, and to meditate upon her unexpected passing. Mom lived her volitional conscientiousness to the end of her life, with an obsessive, enlightened, adoration for her children and grandsons. There we were, framed pictures of all of us prominently staged throughout her daily conversations as an early-onset Alzheimer's patient in an all-White memory care facility in southwest Virginia. Mom paradoxically had to now abide within the circumstance that top quality health care still remained calculatedly segregated. As a patient, perhaps she was forgiven for her "transgressions" because she was so highly respected in the region. Perhaps the vigilance of my brother and I to demand her comfort and care were confounding and unyielding recriminations to the staff that love could not be pigeonholed neatly by heritage, because their tears, sorrows and comforts for us were true.

Perhaps my mother was the shrewdest of all providing the capstone lesson of her freedom released in death. She had requested some years prior that we scatter her ashes, rather than bury her next to her parents and last husband, or heed the request of our grieving father to bury her in the ancestral ground of his family plots. Both places were conventionally non-integrated, and hence carried troubling associations to the baggage she carried throughout her life. My mother zealously lived beyond practical theatrics of racial propriety, yet these same undertakings exactingly depleted her bliss. In the end, it seemed I was right back where I started so long ago, with my mother not knowing me, as I held her little body close and kissed her sweet forehead goodnight. My brother has that picture last taken, which I cannot bring myself to look at, knowing she had just asked for the real Michèle to come to her rescue from that place.

Blessed by a most beautiful summer morning, my brother and I surrendered our mother to Appalachian mountain winds, where a favorite stream broke into falling water in the valley where she often rode her horses, happiest and liberated. We made a simple altar of roses for her there.

Although riskily bartered, the circle of my life was healing and closing. I felt that my bargain with God had been fulfilled, as I reflected we had been loyal to each other throughout all error and triumph, even in granting my mother a deserved and untainted final peace. I had come many miles, and now I resignedly anticipated the lullaby of ocean crescendos and cascades to give me sleep, and longed for a spectacular dawn when I arose in the morning. Just as my father had revealed to me when I was a child, the dignity of our practiced faith never disappointed and always restored. I would find my way to live with loss, knowing also that it came with a cost no one but my brother and I would understand, and have to forgive. One last look at the purple horizon from my balcony was a reassuring, breathtaking imprint. I was offered solace and took it from these harbingers of nature all around me, many which defied taming and capture, and perhaps always would, quite like myself. With such a reckoning of contemplation to burnish me, God and I were, finally, good.

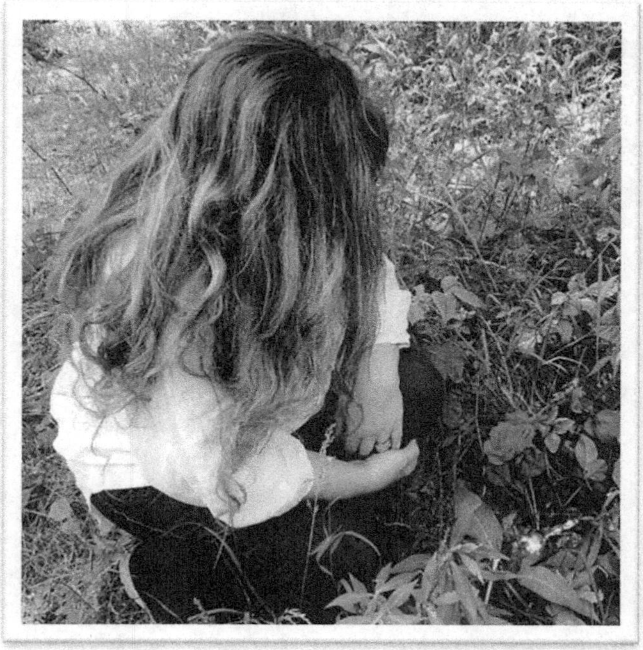

FREEING MOM... FORGIVING OTHERS...

PROLOGUE: QUEEN OF SPADES

Since I must play the cards I've been dealt,
I will play the hand that matters.
So that the fidelity of my work will not be lost,
And my loyalties will not be shattered.
Protectively, I nurture the source of my strength,
And trust even the worst can be endured.
I have realized that within infinite possibility,
Every unexpected joy is assured.
Like a warrior, I've been Affirmed by nature,
With an improbable originality bound by none.
Somehow, I believe this hand I've played,
Is simply my Life,
Undone.

ACKNOWLEDGEMENTS

I would like to thank my expertly critical draft readers, each who encouraged me and provided safe emotional spaces to tell these truths for the benefit of others, affirming for me my vision and true purpose of teaching and healing: Reverend Cecil "Chip" Murray, Barbara "Mom" Langford, Renita Tyson, Wendy Gladney, and of course final approvers Todd Turner, Charisse Turner, Vance Gillenwater and Darnita Gillenwater. Also, I am most blessed with the voices in my Village of Chaz Guest and Tiffani Laidler, who made sure I got it done. It is done.

Note: While each of the "Life Lessons" are actual life experiences, many of the names of people and places have been changed.

ABOUT THE AUTHOR

SHELI TURNER was born in San Francisco, California. She resides in Los Angeles, California with her brilliant husband and phenomenal sons.

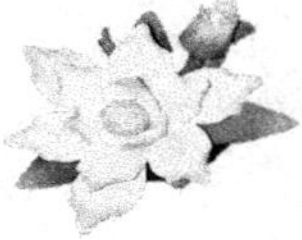

CPSIA information can be obtained
at www.ICGtesting.com
Printed in the USA
BVHW041713220319
543460BV00010B/127/P

9 781732 580602